# Asleep At Work

# PRAISE FOR SHAWN MCCANN'S BOOK
## ASLEEP AT WORK

"Asleep at Work is an interesting perspective on workplace dysfunction, based on author Shawn McCann's testament and attribute of critical awareness. As is revealed in this book, it appears that no workplace genre or culture seems to be immune to compromising employees and employers who manage by bullying, being deceitful or subscribing to stereotypes. The honesty that McCann brings to the text held a mirror for many situations that I had endured while working in professional settings and were affirmations that it "wasn't personal", just business as usual. He examines the challenges and conflicts of the human spirit in employment and shows the possibility of triumph of good character over evil doers. As a professor in conflict analysis, resolution, and management, I applaud the candor of this book and its author and see this book as a primer for those entering or existing in the workplace."

~Dr. Barbara Sunderland Manousso, Ph.D.
CEO and Founder of Manousso Mediation Training
& ADR Services and Mediation Resource Center

"Have you ever felt like there is a disconnect between direct service staff and administrators? Is the culture of your organization one where infighting is more common than teamwork? Do you ever wonder while working...Am I missing something? If you answered yes to one or all of these questions then this book is for you. In Asleep at Work, Shawn McCann creates a

# Asleep At Work

*Thoughts On Surviving In The
Ever-Changing Workplace*

SHAWN P. MCCANN

**BALBOA.**
PRESS

A DIVISION OF HAY HOUSE

ISBN: 978-1-4525-6359-6 (sc)
ISBN: 978-1-4525-6360-2 (e)

Library of Congress Control Number: 2012921786

Balboa Press books may be ordered through booksellers or by contacting:

Balboa Press
A Division of Hay House
1663 Liberty Drive
Bloomington, IN 47403
www.balboapress.com
1-(877) 407-4847

Because of the dynamic nature of the Internet, any web addresses or links contained in this book may have changed since publication and may no longer be valid. The views expressed in this work are solely those of the author and do not necessarily reflect the views of the publisher, and the publisher hereby disclaims any responsibility for them.

The author of this book does not dispense medical advice or prescribe the use of any technique as a form of treatment for physical, emotional, or medical problems without the advice of a physician, either directly or indirectly. The intent of the author is only to offer information of a general nature to help you in your quest for emotional and spiritual well-being. In the event you use any of the information in this book for yourself, which is your constitutional right, the author and the publisher assume no responsibility for your actions.

Any people depicted in stock imagery provided by Thinkstock are models, and such images are being used for illustrative purposes only.
Certain stock imagery © Thinkstock.

Printed in the United States of America

Balboa Press rev. date: 11/20/2012

To my mother the woman who encouraged me to shoot for
the stars and to rise above the rest, "*just like a giraffe*".
All that I am and all that I ever aspire to be I owe to my mother. To
my Dad "Big Earl" for teaching me what perseverance is all about.
To the many whose shoulders I stood on
as a tool of encouragement.

And

To you, the many workers all over the world,
I hope this book makes your life at work less stressful.

# CONTENTS

# ACKNOWLEDGEMENTS

I would like to thank and acknowledge the following people and places for their inspiration and for helping me to find my way: Sara McCann, AB Maurice, Dr. Barbara Huval, Reginald Bush, Henry Mayes, Annette Mitchell, Amy Perro, Johnnie McCann, Starbucks Coffee (a good place to write), Sertino's Café in Port Arthur, TX (a great place to think and write), Anthony Jones, Roderick Gibbs (BMT), Kirk Jones, Andrew, Brandon and Julio Garza and Shawn Gaines.

My staff for keeping me grounded with laughter:

Fred Jones, Annisia Shynett, Beth Camp, Beena Valiaparambil and Ana "Cheska" Delgado

To my siblings: Gregg, Shantel, Shannon, Patrick and Earl Jr.

And

To my daughters, Bailey & Lexi McCann (keep on rising)

# INTRODUCTION

This is not another motivational book about how to win something, defeat someone or how to make a million dollars by *"following these few simple steps"*, nor is it meant to pit employees against their employers; however, it provides some practical thoughts, experiences and applications for dealing with the truth and embracing where you are in the moment at work, and most of all, living and working well. In addition, the content in this book is meant to be insightful for both the employee and the employer, and to help put some perspectives on the dynamics and realties of what often happens in the workplace.

Have you ever felt like you were sleeping during a meeting at work and everyone around you seemed to be alert except for you? I have, you see for me sometimes during meetings my mind usually wandered aimlessly replaying past jobs that I hated and the dream job that I so desperately wanted. I imagined myself in a corporate suite with expensive furniture where everyone was respected and life was really good. I imagined the business trips, the power lunches, important contacts and hob knobbing with the elite. Most of all, I imagined what it would feel like for my wife and children to be incredibly wealthy and comfortable. I'm not talking about being snobbish or fake, but rather the good life, the life filled with wealth that my family would enjoy for generations to come.

Then, I would abruptly hear my boss utter, *"Shawn, would you like to add something"* referring to some aspect of the meeting, and I was always good at adlibbing and very sharp with comebacks. I became so good over the years I would sometimes astonish myself with the bull crap. I would often say, "Yes, you are right on the money with that one, or I concur", sometimes not having a clue as to what the discussion was centered around.

At the time that I started to contemplate writing this book, I worked as a contractor in the Aerospace Industry at NASA in a field called Labor and Employee Relations. I was charged with solving problems and conflicts that employees inevitably experienced on a daily basis. My role was to somehow provide an objective avenue for leaders and staff to seek guidance concerning working conditions, performance issues, misconduct and any other areas of concern. My job also entailed maintaining employer-employee relationships that contributed to satisfactory productivity, motivation and morale. Essentially, my role was concerned with preventing and resolving problems involving individuals that arose out of or affected work conditions. In short, I was a glorified babysitter, or at least it felt that way a lot of times.

One day my journey started with a simple statement, and no it's not *"Houston, we have a problem"*, but rather, *"I don't know what to tell you"*. You see, my mother would always say this very statement to me right after I'd asked for her opinion regarding what I felt at the time was of importance to me; like a certain problem that I was experiencing on the job, perhaps dealing with an annoying co-worker, a dishonest boss or even worse a dishonest executive.

When I was a child, I really didn't understand what my mother was referring to when she often said, *"I don't know what to tell you"* but later on in life throughout my teenage years up to adulthood, I finally understood the meaning of that phrase. Simply put, you can ask ten different people how to become free of something and chances are; you will receive ten different answers. In short, sometimes no one knows exactly what to tell another. An individual must have an understanding of his own surroundings and a spirit of belief that guides him or her in the right direction and/or conclusion concerning any given matter.

When my mother said to me many years ago, *"I don't know what to tell you"*, she was in fact saying "Shawn, you already know the answer, why are you asking the question". This is true for many of us because life is filled with many speed bumps and road blocks and if we keep stopping to ask questions along the way, we lose a sort of metaphorical momentum which slows us down sometimes to a complete and utter halt. Therefore, I say to you, keep on moving just like the hands of time. Whatever it is that you want to do or accomplish in this world with regards to your career, make it happen, and make it happen right now!

Create a vision of what you want in a job or career and call it into existence, the answers will come to you like a thief in the night, when you least expect it. The more you wait and ponder aimlessly, the more time is passing away on your dream job.

This book will examine some thoughts on how to handle the eight plus hours or system that we deal with on a daily basis, also known as work and how to transform that inertia into something that will pleasantly blow you away. In addition, this book will explore a short story scenario that highlights some of the key discussions throughout the chapters and will encourage you to feel good regardless of the current situation that presents itself, *and it will be presented.*

It is my hope that everyone who reads this book can take away some concepts that will lead them to some level or degree of understanding of what they might be experiencing on a daily basis at work and the means in which they can overcome those situations. It has always been my intention and desire to share some knowledge and experiences so as to help others to understand and survive this fundamental and systemic cycle.

The short story (fable) after Chapter 8 is a compilation of events that I have first-hand witnessed, been made privy to and have researched over the years. In addition, and in some regards, it is an anthology of wisdom that many people in the Corporate World, Business World, various Religious Figures, Teachers, Friends and my Parents have shared with me in my personal plight of managing conflict and dealing with different behaviors in the workplace. Most importantly, the ideal situation is within reach of all of us, we just have to ask for it and believe that it is already there, just as the answers to our questions are already there as well.

Merriam Webster defines *sleep* as the natural periodic suspension of consciousness during which the powers of the body are restored. In this same entry, Webster also includes the word *death*, referring to it as a permanent cessation of all vital functions – the end of life. Although death and sleep takes on different meanings, I'm sure that in your lifetime, you've heard someone refer to death as a long sleep or some rendition thereof.

It is amazing that as human beings, we describe things according to the circumstances. Consider this, if you are working for an organization and the pressures, that is to say stress, etc. of being at that organization are too overwhelming; you will surely get sick in your mind, body and spirit or perhaps even all of the above if you remain there. This situation in and of itself is a form of death sort to speak, and most of us at times will choose to remain in dead-end types of jobs instead of doing something about it.

You see, by remaining at an organization that causes stress which usually lends itself to other debilitating issues with the body, keeps one in a constant state of sleep and is a very ridiculous notion to say the least. If you are currently experiencing a situation at work that is causing a great deal of stress or otherwise, I would encourage you to wake up out of this state of death because you have been asleep for far too long and it's time to enjoy the work that you do, while you still can.

A good friend of mine suffered multiple strokes as a result of worry, stress and frustration of working for companies that literally made him sick. Now, in the normal, you would think that someone who suffered one stroke as a result of being frustrated would have done something to prevent future strokes, since a stroke can be lethal. Needless to say, my childhood friend has been confined to a wheelchair since his late thirties, which is a very young age.

Strokes in general are unpredictable and usually happen suddenly. According to information on WebMD, general symptoms of stroke include: sudden numbness, tingling, weakness or loss of movement in your face, arm or leg, especially on only one side of your body. Other symptoms include sudden vision changes, sudden trouble speaking, sudden confusion or trouble understanding simple statements, sudden problems with walking or balance, sudden severe headaches, etc. and the list goes on and on.

The point to all of this is rather simple, knowing what could happen if you remain in a debilitating situation, why on earth would you continue to work in a situation that fosters stress and unhappiness instead of doing something that would make you feel good both mentally and physically.

*"Life is a comedy for those who think and*
*a tragedy for those who feel."*

~Horace Walpole

# Chapter 1

# Are You Hurt or Are You Injured

M Y EIGHTH GRADE FOOTBALL COACH would always say to a player that was slow getting up after being tackled by another player, *"Are you hurt or are you injured"*. If a player was hurt that meant that he needed a quick breather and would go back into the game shortly; however, if a player was injured, that meant that he would most likely be out for the remainder of the football season.

These seven words that my coach said to players on a daily basis indelibly stayed on my mind throughout the years during my personal experiences in life as well as experiences and challenges at work. Whenever I found myself in a tough situation to include work, relationships, college or whatever, I would always ask myself, am I hurt or am I injured, and I've always chosen to be hurt because that reminded me that my situation and how I felt about it, albeit was temporary.

When I was in the fifth grade, one day my life changed forever. I remember being at a weekly Cub Scout meeting and after the meeting, I joined some of my fellow Cub Scouts in what I considered at that time to be a few innocuous games of marbles. The game of marbles was very simple to me, I remember the joy that I would get whenever I would either shoot at another opponent's marble taking them out of the game, thereby increasing my chances of winning more marbles or at best winning all of the marbles.

However, on this particular day, the year was 1981, around five o'clock PM after a routine cub scout meeting after school, I remember that it was a warm day, with a brisk breeze in the air and the sun appeared to be shining on me because I was winning while playing marbles with some of my friends, and I felt like the President of Marbles Incorporated because after all, isn't that what corporate moguls do, beat everyone out of their marbles. It was the very essence of that particular game of marbles that ultimately started the process of enlightenment for me.

It was on that day, in the fifth grade, that a teacher, not ours I might add, approached us in the middle of a game and said to us, *"Boys, go home it's getting late"*, and I along with my friends uttered disrespectful remarks, under our breaths of course, and pretended to walk as though we were going home. However, when that teacher drove passed us on her way home, we waited for several minutes until she had driven out of our sights and proceeded to play marbles again. That's all that I can recall about that particular day.

The next thing that I remembered was opening my eyes and my vision was really blurred by all of the machines and people that I didn't recognize. Suddenly, I heard a familiar voice and it was my mother saying to me *"It's going to be okay"*. Soon afterwards, I recalled trying to get up from what I thought was my bed at home to get ready for school. To my surprise, I learned that I was hit by a drunk driver the previous day while walking home from that game of marbles.

I stayed in the hospital for several weeks which felt like an eternity and upon my release I stayed at home for additional weeks for rehabilitation to recover from my near death injuries that I had sustained from that drunk driver's car. My skull was fractured, my hip was fractured and a part of my left leg was fractured. Although I had missed a significant amount of time from school, my fifth grade teacher, Mrs. Coleman, came to my home everyday to deliver the lesson plan that she had disseminated earlier to my classmates so that I would stay on task with the rest of my classmates.

It wasn't until years later that I would learn from my mother the extent of what actually happened the day that I was hit by the drunk driver. My mother tearfully explained to me that not only was I hit by the car, but I was also attached by my shirt to the driver's car and pulled a short distance. My Cub Scout uniform was ripped to shreds. My mother kept my Cub Scout uniform for many years and one day showed it to me so that I would know and understand just how lucky I was to be alive.

When I was in the fifth grade, I remembered going to several neurologist, but at the time I wasn't aware of what a neurologist actually practiced and/or performed on patients. Later in life, my mother explained to me that she was informed by one of my doctors that I might have some problems in school that would cause me at best to be in remedial classes and that I would most likely have difficulties throughout my educational career and life for that matter.

My mother in the spirit of persistency and tenacity was not going to allow that to happen to her son, in fact, she pushed me every step of the way to learn with vigor. My mother instilled in me and my siblings a great deal of tenacity and made us understand that education would permeate every aspect of our lives, and it was her attitude about education and strong belief in me that made me realize that it was important for me to achieve academically despite the injuries that I had sustained during that drunk driver incident. My mother would often quote famous people particularly those who in some form or fashion made a difference and lasting impression on the lives of others despite their perceived misfortunes and circumstances.

Throughout the years, I've often thought about that game of marbles and how I am blessed that my life was spared and I truly know that my life's work here on earth is not finished, that I might be a source of encouragement and help to others. Shortly after receiving my Master's Degree in Behavioral Science from the University of Houston, I was able to put that particular game of marbles when I was in the fifth grade into perspective. The teacher in the fifth grade who told me and my friends to go home represented wisdom, authority and most of all security because during those times, for most of us, teachers represented a figure in addition to our parents who actually cared about us and our well being. The drunk driver represented a turning point in my life, a sort of reminder of what could and sometimes will happen to a person who is defiant and disrespectful to their elders and who rejects wisdom, in this particular case, the wisdom from someone who had already traveled the road that I was on. My scars from that injury represented a lifelong reminder of my journey that would be filled with change, obstacles and decisions, especially as it related to my career. In fact, the injury to my skull left a permanent scar that is visible to everyone this very day.

Today, in spite of the sometimes arduous journey and obstacles in my life that I have overcome, I sometimes have moments at work when I am truly disgusted with how people have little and sometimes no regards for how others feel. Make no mistake about it, we all have feelings, be it anger, sadness, happiness, frustration, joy, so forth and so on; and when you cease to have some sort of feeling at any given time, you are dead, literally. Nevertheless, despite my frustrations at times, I am generally and genuinely happy with my career and my ability to perform well within it.

Even when life sends me a few curve balls or bumps, I try to remain focused and sustain some level of joy. When I think of those bumps as a metaphor to slowing something or someone down, I often remember one of the best presents that I've ever received. When I graduated from high school in 1989, a friend of mine received a book titled *The University of Hard Knocks* written by Ralph Parlette as a graduation present and later shared the book with me. After reading the book several times throughout the years, I felt and still feel that this is an incredible book, the analogies, morals and metaphors in this book are very meaningful, insightful and priceless.

Two of my favorite quotes from *The University of Hard Knocks* simply put are "There are two kinds of people, wise people and fools. The fools are the people who think they have graduated" referring to knowing all there is to know about life. The other quote, "The tuition in the University of Hard Knocks is not free…Experience is the dearest teacher in the world". For me, these simple phrases have provided answers to a lifetime of problems, especially those problems that are often prevalent in the workplace. You see, in this book, Ralph Parlette refers to knocks as reminders of something that we are doing wrong and lessons that perhaps we can learn from those knocks, hence the tale that follows.

## THERE'S AN OPENING IN MY DEPARTMENT

Remember, people often can hurt your feelings or emotions, but they can never injure your feelings or emotions unless you allow them to do so. I'll never forget, in 2009, I was approached by a young lady in tears whom I will refer to simply as "E" who was new to the Company that I was working for. E was an Attorney who worked in the Recruiting department and I worked in the Labor and Employee

Relations department. Both of these departments were entities within the Human Resources department.

I had several friends including the recruiting manager that worked in the recruiting section and I would often visit them to discuss news, sports and other interests that we had in common. Although I was friends with the recruiting manager, we often kept that a secret so as to minimize against any misconceptions within the department. While visiting the recruiting office one day, I noticed that E was in tears; and I asked her what was wrong and she informed me that she could no longer work in the recruiting department because of the manager.

At that moment, I was placed in a real dilemma because the recruiting manager was not only my colleague, but also my friend. Nevertheless, my job was responsible for addressing all sorts of issues, even if those issues included employees in my own department. Therefore, I scheduled some time to meet with E so that I could better understand her concerns.

When the day came for E and me to meet, E informed me that she wanted to reschedule the meeting because she was scared and had concerns of retaliation from her boss who was my friend and colleague. I assured E that the Company did not allow employees to retaliate against someone for bringing forward concerns and subsequently we met.

During the meeting E became very emotional while describing a vivid array of concerns to include experiencing harassment and being bullied by her boss. E became so emotional and scared that I decided to stop the meeting and rescheduled it for a later date. E also explained that she needed time off from work to assess the situation and would provide more details regarding her plight when she returned.

Although the alleged offender was my friend, I was an agent of the company, and therefore had a due diligence to conduct a thorough investigation into the concerns. After meeting with everyone in the recruiting department including my friend, I could not substantiate any of E's allegations. As a matter of fact, everyone seemed completely shocked by the allegations and could not believe that they were being interviewed.

In addition, most of the employees that I interviewed during the investigation informed me that prior to the investigation, E had informed several of them that she was unhappy and would either be leaving the company soon or would be trying to move to another department. It was even rumored that E had planned a scheme to include fabricating a complaint so that my friend would be investigated and terminated.

The next day I received a call from my boss expressing concerns that the investigation into the matter was taking too long and that I needed to wrap things up. In my haste, I failed to discuss the concerns with my boss over the puzzling information that I had learned in the interviews about E wanting to move to another department and the fact that the investigation was taking long had to do with E's emotional state. Therefore, instead of investigating the situation further, I suggested moving E to my department since there was an opening and a shortage of personnel in the Labor and Employee Relations section and this move would certainly protect the organization from future risks. My boss agreed with my assessment and E started to work in my department. For the next two years, I endured a hostile work environment to include being backstabbed, my work being tampered with and a host of other incredulous behavior all of which I felt and still feel were carefully orchestrated by E from the very start.

That experience taught me a valuable lesson something that I could not have learned from the best schools or teachers in the world. I learned that you must always follow your instincts and be very careful of the people that cry wolf sort to speak. It is also important to examine the smallest of details, for that may be the very thing that causes your demise at work.

Moral of the story, be careful of trusting others, sometimes a smiling face is just a frown turned upside down. As I was growing up and matriculating through school, my mother often talked to me by using what she often referred to as *"old sayings"*. One of my favorite old sayings from my mother was to *"Keep your friends close and keep your enemies in your back pocket"*. Translation – You must always know what your enemy is doing. According to Sun Tzu, *The Art of War*, "If you know the enemy and know yourself, you need not fear the result of a hundred battles. If you know yourself but not the enemy, for every victory gained you will also suffer a defeat. If you know neither the enemy nor yourself, you will succumb in every battle." Although Sun Tzu was said to be a brilliant military general who lived in China during the 6th Century BC, I think that his insight and tactics on warfare can be used in our daily lives to help us maneuver through the bureaucracy at work.

I'm not suggesting that employees and employers should fight each other in a military style battle; however, what I am suggesting is that all individuals must understand what's going on around them so that they can adequately address situations. This is true of the employee as well as the employer. In some cases employees are bad and in some cases employers are bad. Just as in some cases employees are good and employers are good. I'm referring to when one party is good and the other party is bad, you must know your opponent, if not, it can be very costly to you.

In short, sometimes I think about how funny life is and how often many of us take its very essence for granted. Every day I try to laugh more and often at the things that I do and see at work, the people and systems that I encounter at work and I smile every morning that I wake up because I am happy that I am healthy and that I have a wonderful career, friends and most of all – family. Therefore,

I say to you, whatever circumstances that you might find yourself in at any given time at work, choose to be hurt in that particularly moment and believe that all things are possible and that negative circumstances, people or whatever you might be experiencing at work, are only temporary.

*"I am the thinker that creates the thoughts
that creates the things."*

~ Dr. Johnnie Coleman

# Chapter 2

# Find Your Passion At Work

D O YOU KNOW YOURSELF? I mean do you really know who you are? This is an age old question, and has been examined by many scholars, philosophers and theologians alike. In the words attributed to Socrates in Plato's Apology, The Greek Philosopher Socrates in all of his philosophical greatness simply said, *"Know thyself"* and exclaimed that the *"Unexamined life is not worth living"*. Just as with life, do you really know what you want in a job or career? Many of us spend a great deal of time talking about what we want to achieve in a job or career, but never seem to do it. One thing that I've learned over the years is that we cannot just talk about what we want in career, but rather we must have an absolute and specific image of the job and call it into existence. I will discuss the process of bringing a career or job of your liking into existence in Chapter 7 when I discuss the importance of believing. For now, please consider the following:

## PASSION STARTS FROM A PURPOSE OR A VISION

A few years ago, I went to a human resources conference and the keynote speaker was discussing how everyone within an organization contributes to the vision of the organization. The vision of an organization is typically a result of its mission. Put another way, for example, if an organization's mission is to *"Provide resources, food, etc. to an underserved population, etc."* then its vision might be *"A population living up to its potential, etc."* or something to that effect.

The speaker explained that in 1961, President Kennedy set a goal of putting a man on the moon by the end of that decade. As a result, a panel from the U.S. Congress became so involved with the President's goal that they decided to visit Houston, Texas, the hub for the space industry and space travel. While visiting the then Manned Spacecraft Center now Johnson Space Center, a Congressman saw a man sweeping in one of the buildings and asked him, "Excuse me sir, what is your job", and it was reported that the man sweeping replied to the Congressman, "To get a man on the moon". Needless to say, that particular individual was not directly responsible for getting a man on the moon via any of his job duties as a custodian; however, it was the sheer passion of President Kennedy's goal of getting to the moon that translated to everyone at NASA the vision of going to the moon regardless of their specific job title. This goal ultimately became not only a vision, but a very successful program.

## BECOME THE GREATEST OF ALL TIMES

It's one thing to be good at something and another to strive at being excellent; however, both of these ideas have a short shelf life.

Safe! You can't go wrong with striving for excellence. Being excellent is what mostly everyone strives to be, until a better person comes along. However, being the greatest of all times is something quite unique and everlasting.

One day while sitting at my desk at work, I was listening to a motivational recording by Les Brown, the renowned motivational speaker and author. This recording was given to me by a friend and colleague. I recall having a really difficult time at work and my friend insisted that I listen to Les Brown. At that time, I was the consummate skeptic when it came to motivational speakers, inspirational readings and the likes.

I listened to Les Brown's recordings multiple times, I even had my friend to dub me a copy so that I could use it at home. I started listening to the recordings every day and became so familiar with its content that I started mimicking the words to relatives, friends, acquaintances and anyone else who would listen to me. This recording was truly a gem in that it provided simple strategies to address problems and daily struggles. Les Brown spoke about being the greatest in your field at work and how to transform your life.

Although I had listened to Les Brown's recordings over and over, one day while struggling tremendously at work with all of the office bureaucracy, it came to me like an explosion. I remembered Les Brown saying on one of his segments, something to the effect "What are you willing to do to succeed?" At that moment, I decided that everything that I did then and in the future, I was going to be the best. It was one of those awakenings like in the movie 'The Matrix' by the Wachowski Brothers, starring actor Keanu Reeves. I was posed with a question, for which I already knew the answer, just like when I used to ask my mother certain questions and she would reply, "I don't know what to tell you". In the movie, 'The Matrix', the character Neo played by Keanu Reeves deals with the constant theme of understanding choices, dealing with various choices and the consequences of those choices.

I love this movie, as well as the subsequent releases that comprised its trilogy. It demonstrates an awakening of sorts which delves the main character into contemplating perspectives on his new found realities about life. You see, we all have to make decisions with regards to our jobs and careers, and in doing so, you too will discover new found realities about your job as well. However, while contemplating decisions and perspectives about your job, you should always consider becoming the greatest in your profession, career, job, etc. Dr. Martin Luther King, Jr. once said *"If you're called to be a street sweeper, be the best"*. To illustrate this point, I would first like to ask the questions; what are you willing to do to succeed? And what are you willing to give up? Like me, I'm sure that you've heard people say that they would do just about anything to get a particular job, position, career, etc. But have you noticed only a very small percentage of the world's population is very successful and wealthy.

This is not by mistake or accident. I will admit, some people have received their wealth through inheritance, but this too is through someone else's doing something to achieve the wealth in order to leave to their heirs in the first place. In addition, there are those who have received their fortunes through serendipity; however, this too is extremely rare and is often times the work of others as well.

Achievement and ultimate success in your job, craft, profession, etc. depends on you and your commitments. For example, let's talk about 16 year old gymnast, Gabby Douglas and her performance at the 2012 Olympics in London which made her instantly a part of a small sorority comprised of the world's greatest female gymnasts. However, prior to becoming one of the greatest, she had to do the impossible which entailed moving away from her family and hometown of Virginia Beach, also away from everything that was familiar to her in a quest for greatness. Further, this meant moving to Iowa for two years to harness her skills as a gymnast. It was also reported that during these two years, she only saw her family four times. I'm almost certain that during these two years away from her family, she must have endured many lonely days, all in an effort to be the greatest. Given those circumstances, I don't know of too many 16 year olds or any other age groups for that matter that would move across country to work at becoming the best at anything. The pressures and commitments are far too strenuous for most.

Speaking of Olympic greatness, it goes without saying, and deservingly so that swimmer Michael Phelps is the most decorated and perhaps the greatest Olympian of all times. Like most Olympians, Michael Phelps started his venture at a very young age and honed his skills with the help of his coach Bob Bowman. Imagine for a moment that at a very young age you would have to forego hanging out with friends, doing other typical things that teenagers engage in, all in an effort to be the greatest. Again, I say to you, that if asked, most people would not be willing to give up much; the pressures and commitments are far too much to bear. Success costs and you have to know with exact certainty the amount you are willing to pay for it.

At the London Olympic Games, Michael Phelps made a reference to Michael Jordan as being someone he admired and for being the best in his sport. Needless to say, Michael Jordan is the greatest basketball player of all times and Phelps joins Jordan as the greatest in history at his sport, swimming. More importantly, it was Michael Jordan's passion for the game and commitment to being the best that ultimately made him the greatest basketball player.

I once read that Michael Jordan played in a game while having flu like symptoms and despite doctors orders, Jordan played 49 minutes and scored a game high 38 points, to beat the Utah Jazz 90-88. Not many of us would contemplate working while having flu like symptoms. Now, I'm not suggesting that anyone should go to work sick, that wouldn't be smart; however, you get the point.

Also, learn from successful people in your field or in general, as to how they became successful. If asked, I'll bet that the theme of commitment, passion, focus and other synonymous descriptors would be at the forefront of their ingredients for success. At the onset of the segment in this chapter, I asked the questions, what are you willing to do to succeed and what are you willing to give up. To illustrate this point, if you haven't seen the movie 'The Pursuit of Happyness' starring Will Smith you really should check it out. The movie is based on the real life story of Chris Gardner (CEO of his own Stockbrokerage Firm) and his nearly one year struggle with homelessness. This movie epitomizes the spirit of commitment and what one is capable of doing once their mind is made up. It is probably safe to say that most successful people have struggled somewhat to get to the top. Struggling is only temporary when you have decided what it is that you want in a career. I once read somewhere that if you know the reasons for wanting something, then you can overcome almost any how when it comes to getting it.

## SURVIVAL OF THE HAPPIEST

Remember, not only should you surround yourself with positive people and read positive literature, but the most important ingredient of all is happiness. You may have heard that only the strongest can survive or that ultimate survival depends on the fittest. These statements are true; however, if you think about it, those strong and fit people are often times happy as well, in a sense, happiness is the key to their success at work. In an article blog in *Forbes*, *Happier Employees are More Productive and More Innovative*; read, "The driving force behind workplace positive psychology is the notion that happier employees are more productive, more innovative, and create a more attractive working environment."

Some years ago, I was flying back home from a work related conference and I recalled that the flight was filled with me constantly thinking of being very tired and begrudged about the success of others within my organization and the idea of having to go to work the next day didn't make the trip any better. To make matters even worse, I was sitting in the middle seat between two annoying passengers listening to the person on my left and the person on my right complain to each other about their jobs as if it were their life's work to complain. Suddenly, out of nowhere, I started to feel better, I even felt somewhat sorry for those individuals whom I had the pleasure of being annoyed by nearly the entire flight home. To me, the thought of complaining about something that you have to deal with everyday; such as work, couldn't be healthy for anyone, what a horrible feeling. Think about it, for most of us, work is our bread and butter sort to speak and the place that we spend most of our time. Therefore, it is necessary that you change your attitude mentally and revel in the fact that you have a job to go to. Your current situation is temporary, so enjoy it until you can physically move on to the next chapter in your work life.

I have read many books and researched countless topics on the laws of attraction, belief and thought processes. Put simply, you become what you think about and talk about most of the time. In short, your words and thoughts become your experiences. Therefore, if you are not happy about going to work and are constantly thinking and saying that you are not happy, then guess what? Chances are; you will not be happy at work and you will forever talk about your unhappiness. I think that you will be very surprised to know that if you change your thought process to being happy at work, then your experiences will be better.

Recent research has shown that happiness levels can be increased with minimum amount of effort. Professor Sonja Lyubomirsky of the University of California Riverside and author of *The How of Happiness*; has conducted happiness research with thousands of men and women. Among her conclusions: A full 40 percent of your happiness level is completely within your control. You may have received unhappy genes and suffered unfortunate life circumstances, but you still have a clean 40 percent at your command.

While researching the topic of being happy at work, I ran across an article in *Science Daily* which literally jumped off the page as I was reading. The caption read, *"People who are unhappy in life are unlikely to find satisfaction at work."* I thought this message was incredible because not only should you be happy at work, the trick is to permeate happiness in every walk of life possible so as to generate positive experiences into your life. Remember, you become what you think about and talk about most of the time; therefore, discuss being happy and more importantly, show it, live it and sing it. Ralph Waldo Emerson (Essayist, Poet and Lecturer) once said "Enthusiasm is one of the most powerful engines of success. When you do a thing, do it with all your might. Put your whole soul into it. Stamp it with your own personality. Be active, be energetic and faithful, and you will accomplish your objective. Nothing great was ever achieved without enthusiasm."

Bobby McFerrin (vocalist), best known for his 1988 hit song *"Don't Worry, Be Happy"*, transformed the lives of many people all over the world. It became a theme song for some and a mantra for many alike struggling in life as well as work. You must tell yourself that regardless of the circumstances at work, "I am happy that I have a job and I am ready to change my circumstances at work". In addition to having a positive demeanor, you must act on your thoughts. Being happy alone can only get you so far.

Speaking of which, I also came across an article in the *Harvard Business Review*, *"How to Be Happier at Work"*, which discussed being action oriented. According to this particular article, "The key is to start, to take a small step toward what you think you want." Can you recall going to work for a company that you thought was the best thing since sliced bread? Or better yet, can you recall what it was like on your first day of orientation at a new job, the nervousness about something new and the excitement for what you could become in this new venture. You see, that was the essence of being happy, because in some cases you had just left a bad situation, position, job, company, etc. Now, fast forward years later, the new situation is now once again the bad situation. And once again, how do you feel? Not happy of course. This will inevitably be a never ending cycle of temporary fixes if you don't solve the problem. In short, the problem is not totally the job, the system, your coworkers, it's YOU. You have to fix *you* before you can move on to something better.

Several years ago, my wife and I were perusing the latest and greatest Best Seller's list at the book store and we came across a book called *The Secret*, by Rhonda Byrne. Now, I must admit, I was a huge skeptic when it came to change, growth or "how to" books, etc. considering that I was an acute worry wart at one point in my life. I worried about everything from my career to who I thought was going to win a particular sporting event. One would have thought that I was indebted to the Mafia because I worried so much.

However, this book by Rhonda Byrne was so intense and transformational, that I literally could not go to sleep once I started reading it. It was as if the information within the book was the metaphorical part of the puzzle that my life had been missing up to that point. The information that was disseminated by Rhonda Byrne and other contributors in *The Secret* was so profound that I literally felt energized and immediately happy. I wanted to read this book all the time so I also bought the CD of the book so that I could listen to it while I was driving to work or running other errands. I eventually bought the DVD so that I could see the contributors talk about their segments and to pretend that they were speaking directly to me. I was really happy when I read, listened to the CD or watched the DVD. This book was truly a gift and a very inspirational message and a good secret that I discovered.

Now, I'm not talking about the type of happiness that one might experience from being told that they have just won a hundred million dollars from the lottery. I'm referring to the joy and inner peace that one feels when they have received information and solutions to help them change negative or ineffective thought processes that have taken over their lives for so many years or have guided them into a system of unhappiness, stress, anger, resentment or other destructive measures; particularly those which affect ones demeanor and ability to perform well at work.

Prior to reading *The Secret*, I was very miserable and tired of the Company that I was working for at the time. I was at the brink of quitting my job; however, that really wasn't an option at the time considering that my family needed me. I remember reading *The Secret* and watching how not only my personal life unfolded, but my experiences at work became so tremendously better that everyone thought that I had either found out that I was dying and decided to be happy the rest of my days or that I had been on some type of drug. However, to the contrary, I had just discovered something so powerful that everyone noticed it through my actions.

Remember, happiness is a choice and I try to exude as much happiness as I can possibly muster at work, even if the situation is seemingly unbearable. Also, I would highly recommend that you study people that are successful in the field of work that you would like to be in, read material and become a student on the details of the job that you want and imagine that the job is already yours. Become happy about it, even if it hasn't materialized yet. I can assure you that if you claim it, the job is on its way to you. Not only did the principles that I learned through reading *The Secret* make me a better person, but it also attracted me to other books, people and experiences that have left a profound feeling within me that I wouldn't be able to describe in a billion words.

In short, surround yourself with motivational and inspirational things (*i.e., books, music, quotes, etc.*) on a daily basis and never,

never, never, allow anyone to steal your happiness you are ultimately responsible for your happiness. Harriet Beecher Stowe (Teacher and Author) once said, *"Never give up, for that is just the place and time that the tide will turn."* Therefore, you must be committed to being happy first and foremost, in order for your situation at work to change.

A few years ago while visiting some friends; I noticed that they had a picture in their living room of a very old gentleman who looked very sickly. Alongside the picture was a caption which read:

First, I was dying to finish high school and start college
And then I was dying to finish college and start working
Then I was dying to marry and have children
And then I was dying for my children to grow
old enough so I could go back to work
But then I was dying to retire
And now I am dying...
And suddenly I realized
I forgot to live

Please don't let this happen to you
Appreciate your current situation
And enjoy each day

...old friend

I thought that this was an incredible example of what many of us experience throughout our lives. We forget to enjoy the journey while we still can. On that same picture another caption read: *"To make money we lose our health, and then to restore our health we lose our money. We live as if we are never going to die, and we die as if we never lived."* Wow, this was truly an awakening moment for me.

*"To sin by silence when we should protest*
*makes cowards of men."*

~ ELLA WHEELER WILCOX

# CHAPTER 3

# UNDERSTANDING INSTITUTIONAL DENIAL

I T IS VERY DIFFICULT TO find a company that is genuinely honest these days considering the notion that more and more leaders of organizations are refusing to believe when something terribly wrong is happening within the ranks of their organizations; despite having all of the real signs and evidence to the contrary that is often times presented to them through employee complaints. Now, I'm not suggesting that CEO's should drop everything that they are working on to deal with every employee complaint; however, what I am suggesting is that CEO's alike step out of the executive suites from time to time and take a real climate assessment of their organizations. Some executives might say that *"We've hired this firm or that consulting firm to measure XYZ at the company."* And most of the time, this yields the same old thing from most consulting firms, *"You guys are doing fine, but need to work on your ...",* and for a few bucks more, the consulting firm may find more evidence of things that you need to work on so that you can continue this never ending cycle of paying for their services of finding things that your organization needs to work on.

Also, I would like to make it perfectly clear that I am not bashing or negating the services of all consulting firms; especially those who are really focused on providing the best solutions for companies rather than running up tabs recommending solutions that will never yield the necessary benefits that organizations need. Having said that, it is wise for CEO's to become imbedded in the furtherance and sustainability of their organizations. This means, taking a proactive approach to understanding the men and women who are working on the front lines day in and day out and in most cases, are not making a lot of money doing it.

These statements are very true and powerful and I'm most certain that many of you reading this book can identify with what I'm referring to now and throughout this chapter. This chapter is of huge importance for executives and others in leadership roles in that it provides insight into what leaders of company's often think is going on with regards to concerns in daily operations and what is actually happening in most cases. To illustrate this point please consider the following segments and stories:

## EMPLOYEES AND SYSTEMS

An Employee typically works for another person or organization for pay. A System on the other hand, is any formulated, regular, or special method or plan of procedure. Sounds simple right? Not at all, you see, an employee can and often does disrupts procedures. However, the onus is not always on the employee, the organization is ultimately responsible for the actions of their employees.

In essence, people make up systems and it is essential that leadership in organizations work on improving people in an effort to safeguard good systems. Often times, people come and go and systems remain the same. If the system is ineffective, in most cases the organization suffers. In some cases employees become frustrated and engage in dishonest practices, along with a host of other potential concerns especially if the organization is sales oriented this could be very detrimental to their profit margin. In short, organizations alike may consider focusing on people and not systems. For if you have happy employees; the systems will fall into place almost perfectly.

This leads me to a lesson that I will never forget with regards to systems and employees that I learned many years ago while working for a car rental company in Houston. At the time, I was a recent college graduate and my job prospects were very limited since most of my prior years were spent in school, I lacked the work experience that a lot of company's required. However, it was one company that recruited at college campuses with the notion of finding raw talent for their Management Trainee Program. The idea of this company was to put college graduates into the trainee program with the hopes of developing them into managers so that they could ultimately manage one of the many branches dominated by this company in the rental car retail industry.

By all intents and purposes, this was a fantastic opportunity for me because I had the college degree, the passion and the talent, all except for the experience. Nevertheless, I applied for the job and was accepted into the Management Trainee Program. As a new employee, I became successful almost overnight and within a year's time, I was promoted to manager and was in charge of several staff members. I remember thinking, life was good and I was on my way to the top, or at least I thought I was. First, I would like to digress for a brief moment.

I grew up in a very tight nit and honest household; we were brought up the old fashion way which involved doing what was right and not taking the easy road as I would often hear from my parents as well as teachers in my earlier years. The very essence of doing good things has always had a special place in my heart as well as in my actions. Every time that I'm presented with the opportunity to help someone, I always try to do the right thing.

When I was in college, I worked for a department store selling clothes and other items in the men's department. This particular store is a well known chain which sales many well known brands at the normal highest price possible. However, every other week the store would claim to have a sale on some of those high cost items that were always seemingly in demand. Needless to say, I would always inform customers that came into the store before the sale, that if they would be willing to wait a couple of days, the items that they were purchasing on a particular day would be on sale and that they would save sometimes ten percent or more on the items. Nevertheless, the customers were so happy and couldn't believe that I was giving them tips on saving money, because after all, my job was to make money.

Parts of my sales were commission based which meant that my salary depended on what I sold to customers. The higher the cost of the item meant that I would get more money. With this in mind, it would appear to be a no brainer in terms of selling high ticketed items at the regular price. However, I wanted customers to save money because I too was a customer and I would have wanted someone to look out for my best interests as well. In short, I stayed true to saving customers money while my coworkers fought all of the time over sales often ending friendships to make a buck. I on the other hand, would always win sales rep of the month which meant an extra bonus check for me.

I wanted to share this story because it segues beautifully into what I would later learn while working for that rental car company and later lessons throughout my life. There were several things that I discovered while working for the rental car company that I didn't like nor did I agree with. However, there was one thing in particular that ultimately caused me to quit working for that company.

I loved working in sales and was quite good at the business aspects of selling items and services to people. However, my upbringing would not allow me to cheat and/or mislead people. At the rental car company, we had a requirement to sell damage waiver insurance to customers who rented cars from us as a means to protect the company's property, but really it was just another opportunity for the company to make money. This requirement meant that if your sales were consistently low, you would ultimately be terminated. With the thought of being fired and the constant pressures of selling damage waiver lingering over our heads, a lot of employees became ill and some left the company. It became so brutally competitive, employees were literally lying to customers and manipulating contracts so that it would appear that they sold the damage waiver insurance to customers, I mean it was a real nightmare of sorts.

Now, what most people renting cars from this company or any other rental car company for that matter, didn't know is that if they had insurance on their personal vehicles, then they could use that to cover any potential damages on the rental car thereby rendering our added insurance useless. The employees were well aware of this fact, but we were not allowed to share this important information with customers unless they asked, and most didn't ask questions after being scared to death by the rental experience with descriptions and stories of car crashes, death tolls, other misleading statistics, you name it, anything to sell the damage waiver insurance.

Nevertheless, we were required to sell the damage waiver insurance and attended many training sessions with the Regional Vice President or (RVP) whose job it was to manage a region of rental car branches. This meant a lot of money for this individual, basically on the blood, sweat and misleads that we hustled and haggled our customers with on a daily basis. Being a Regional Vice President meant that you grew through the ranks and most of us aspired to be in that role. Our RVP was well versed in sales and understood the business acumen down to a science, but most importantly, he made commission from all damage waiver sales in the region, wow this was a lot of money.

Now, here's where the lesson comes in. One day, I'll never forget that the RVP retired and a few months later, low and behold he walked into my branch. Keep in mind this was a very wealthy and influential guy. We were on a first name basis, my name is Shawn, but while working for the company he often called me Shane, no harm done, close enough right? Anyway, I came out of my office and explained to one of my new Management Trainees that I would be assisting the gentlemen and explained that he in fact was the former RVP. Everyone eyes dropped with awe, I asked the former RVP how were things going in retirement and he stated with a big smile that *"things were going well"*, but that he needed to rent a car because his wife had been in a fender bender a few days prior.

As I was going through the rental contract with the RVP, we discussed the success of my branch as well as the company as a whole. I automatically added the damage waiver insurance because after all I was sitting in the presence of the RVP who years earlier trained me in the art of selling damage waiver insurance. Needless to say, this was one time that I didn't have to give a spill about how good an idea it was for the renter to buy the damage waiver coverage. After I'd finish typing the rental contract, I purposefully gave him a free car upgrade at no additional cost; I was honored to be helping such an incredible business person. Before I could shake his hand, he informed me emphatically that he didn't need the damage waiver, in fact, his exact words were, *"I won't be needing the damage waiver because I just sent my insurance company a fat check."*

I was shocked to learn that a former RVP who fired employees for having low damage waiver sales didn't want to buy the additional insurance. I really felt like choking this man because after all, I'd put a great deal of effort into working and made a lot of money for that company and I gave them two years of my life. Shortly thereafter, I decided to leave that company for bigger and better things, more importantly for being humiliated through working in denial. Life is filled with lessons and you never stop learning and I learned a valuable lesson from working at that rental car company. Simply put, it's better to be passionate and strive for success on your own terms, instead of giving all of your energy, drive and focus to a company or organization. However, I'm not suggesting that all organizations employ hypocrites to run them; but, you must be very careful in all of your dealings.

Remember that I said that sometimes systems need to be changed in an effort to keep good people. Over ten years later, I walked into one of the branches of that rental car company that I had worked for years earlier to rent a car while on vacation. The manager of the branch rented me the car and as he was getting to the part about damage waiver and by now other added insurance offers, he asked if I wanted the coverage and I said no and he went on to say that I shouldn't worry because my personal insurance would cover the car should something happen to it. Shocked by the revelation, I explained to the manager that I had worked for the same rental car company many years prior. The manager said that the company had changed its requirements for selling damage waiver years earlier due to a focus on employees and a change in priorities. He also explained that many employees spoke out against selling the damage waiver and explained that with so much focus on selling, it impeded their ability to provide good customer service.

I asked the manager if he felt that the employees in the branch were happy and he explained that he had worked under the old regime of selling damage waiver as a requirement and that he was really excited about where the company was headed as a whole and that his branch was leading the region in sales. The moral to all of this is that the system changed, and in doing so, people were happier and the company was even more profitable.

## THE POWER OF SUGGESTION

Suggestion is a very powerful concept and often catches the most intellectual people by surprise if they are not cognitively aware of the deeper meanings behind certain information. Some might say that suggestion is a science of sorts. For example, the human brain is a very intricate organ and has been studied for years by many, but do any of us truly understand or appreciate the power of the human brain. Now, as I have stated before, at one point in my life I was the consummate skeptic until I started reading and thinking about the development of things around me and how those things came to fruition, all from the inception in someone's mind.

When I was working at Johnson Space Center in Houston, I often marveled at the history of space flight and how all of that evolved over the years to include the development of the International Space Station, the iconic walk on the moon, the famous Apollo 13 mission and all of the other things that have occurred within the realms of the aerospace space industry. At first glance, one might not contemplate how or why all of this happened. However, for me, it came to be a simple thought. Someone years ago said to themselves "I can build a spacecraft that could leave earth and venture into space", this is some of the same logic I'm sure must have driven the Wright Brothers into flying. What I'm referring to is the power of suggestion or thought which by its nature propels ideas into action.

The type of suggestion that I'm referring to is more than inferences or propositions, but rather a deeper seated transformation of thoughts into action. I remember when I was in the eighth grade and my basketball coach would always say to us in the locker room just before every game started, *"You are all winners, you can do this and you have already won the game."* Now to most, that would seem strange to have already won a basketball game or anything for that matter considering that we were still in the locker room and the game hadn't even started. However, years later it hit me and really made me think about why my eighth grade basketball coach said the same thing over and over before each game, it wasn't because he thought that we didn't hear him all of the other times, it was his way of suggesting that we would indeed win every game despite our opponents will to beat us. And you know what, we did just that, we won every game.

This same power permeates every aspect of our lives regardless of the event such as work, school, sports, politics, you name it. To illustrate this further, my coach not only used the incantation of informing us that we would win every game, but he often wrote the same statements and placed them throughout the locker room so that we had a constant reminder and mental picture of what he was suggesting to us. This same power asserts itself in the workplace and is often at the behest of leadership without the masses knowing or even understanding.

To illustrate how suggestion is used in organizations, consider that most organizations alike control business objectives that goes far beyond mission, vision or even value statements. For example, most of you reading this book work or have worked at an organization that is or was campaigning for something. It could have been something to the metaphorical beat of giving your hard earned money to the company in which you work, this sounds crazy, and it really is. I remember working for this non-profit corporation, I say corporation because there was nothing non-profit about this organization to say the least. Anyway, the President of this particular organization had a campaign each year that entailed employees giving money via payroll deduction to the United Way. Now, let me be very clear, I'm not against the United Way nor have I ever worked for them; in fact, I think that the United Way is an excellent organization and the non-profit organization that I used to work for often received funding from the United Way because of some of the services that we provided to the local community as an organization.

Now, to the good part! The President of that non-profit organization had a yearly campaign which required every employee regardless of their position, to give a certain percentage of their earned salaries to the United Way. Again, not only do I support the United Way's efforts to give in order to uplift communities, but I also gave of my own free will to various organizations and have given money as well as volunteer support to the United Way. However, the President of the non-profit organization made it her business to demand that employees give money to the United Way so that the United Way would in turn give it to our organization. Sounds harmless right? Wrong! Here's how it all worked. The United Way typically gives pledge cards to organizations so that their employees can designate where they would like their payroll deductions donated. For example, let's say that I wanted my money to go towards a particular literacy program, then I would notate that on my pledge card and then those deductions would come from my paycheck and go towards the literacy program of my choice. Sounds simple right? However, my organization's President at the time had an uncanny skill of suggesting that employees give money to our organization. At first blush, this would seem okay considering that the money would be for the organization in which we worked thereby helping us to uplift our own organization; however, the money that our employees designated to the organization to support programs, really supported the executives wallets and purses.

This brings me to another point, to clear the air sort to speak; I want to say that it's perfectly okay to be successful and to make a lot of money as the owner of a business, CEO or whatever the position might entail. However, I do have a major problem when making money is at the expense or exploitation of others, especially when the playing field of work is not leveled fairly or equitably.

This President used slogans such as "building communities…and one organization, one mission, etc." throughout the campaign to get employees to designate their payroll deductions to the organization, we even had a United Way kickoff party. Everywhere employees turned and looked around there was a slogan about giving money to our own organization in effort to build up the community. The only problem with this was that most employees often struggled to make ends meet and never saw the community uplifted. The lesson here is that you must be very careful of what you're supporting, even if it means supporting your own organization monetarily or otherwise.

## PSYCHOLOGICAL MANAGEMENT

Working for an organization in denial is no different from being sane in a mental institution. What's really alarming is the notion of how do we know the difference between sanity and insanity? Put another way, there are many cases in the media where Criminologist and Psychologist alike are called into court to testify on behalf of the plaintiff to demonstrate that a defendant is sane and in these same cases, there are Criminologist and Psychologist alike called into court to testify on behalf of the defendant to render a plea of insanity. In either case, the notion of sanity and insanity can be at best difficult to understand. The same holds for what is viewed as normal behavior in the workplace by some may be viewed by others as being quite abnormal behavior.

Now, I'm not at all suggesting that behaviors shouldn't be questioned when it comes to certain acts of unusual or offensive behavior in the workplace. For example, theft, harassment, discrimination, physical and/or verbal abuse, etc. are examples of behaviors that are obviously objectionable and are against most policies in any given organization. However, the real question is whether, the objectionable behavior can be adequately distinguished by employees from what's considered appropriate behavior. Put another way, are organizations allowing inappropriate behaviors to exist and persist thereby creating a culture dysfunction? This notion is becoming commonplace meaning that CEO's and other executives in organizations are often removed or strategically blocked by various levels of leadership regarding the dirty dealings that occur and/or reported by various sources. To illustrate this example, in larger companies, CEO's may have a leadership structure that resembles something like this: COO, Senior VP, VP, Asst. VP, Director, Asst. Director, Manager, Supervisor, Team Leader so forth and so on. One might ask, with a structure like this, is it reasonable to expect that a CEO would actually know what's happening at his or her organization?

Consider the fact that I've worked in the field of human resources for more than a decade and in that time frame, I've seen, heard and have been made privy to a lot of dirty dealings at various organizations. What I'm referring to by dirty dealings are those inappropriate situations that happen at the expense of employees as a result of working in an environment that is run by what I will refer to as Psychological Management.

Psychological Management is what I consider to be the idea that leadership doesn't necessarily have to be present in order for employees to work in a sort of controlled environment, even if it means doing something wrong. Have you ever witnessed something at work that you felt was not quite right, but were too afraid to speak out against it for the sake of survival? Many of us, if we're honest with ourselves have in fact witnessed many things that we were not totally happy with or for that matter even proud of in the workplace.

For example, one day I was investigating a concern that was brought to my attention by leadership citing that an employee had committed an egregious policy violation; nevertheless, I conducted an investigation which substantiated the policy violation. However, almost one month later, I was contacted by the same manager who had another employee that committed the same egregious policy violation. This was a no-brainer considering that I had investigated and recommended terminating an employee for the same behavior one month prior. However, I was informed by the manager that this particular employee was said to possibly be an acquaintance of someone who was probably friends with someone on the organization's board of directors. Needless to say, I was instructed by let's say, the powers that be, to give this particular employee *a written warning for violating such policy.* Nevertheless, I followed up with the manager and explained that he should possibly meet with his executive level staff member to explain the circumstances. This meeting never took place, end of story.

Again, this behavior is very unfair; however, this is one of numerous examples that often happens on a daily bases at many organizations. The fact of the matter is that many people in leadership roles are reluctant to question upper-management and executive leadership when it comes to such matters. Now, this may seem to be insane to some or at best very inappropriate to others; however, if the environment allows for such behavior, then is it really safe to say that the behavior itself is insane or inappropriate? Maybe it's the culture that's insane and not the acts.

I've seen more and more organizations operating in this fashion, and it creates a culture of fear and anxiety of sorts. I'm not suggesting that all companies and organizations operate in this fashion; however, I do feel that CEO's and other Executives should take a strong inventory of what is really happening inside their workplaces. Some CEO's may be astonished at what's going on in the trenches while others may already know of the dirty dealings. In either case, some perspectives must change for the safety and well-being of the workplace as a whole.

There's one thing that I've learned from this experience and it has stayed with me throughout my career. Simply put, employees love to communicate with each other especially about the wrongdoings or at least what they perceive to be wrongdoings that occur within organizations. Nevertheless, this a growing epidemic which equates to employees filing federal claims with the Equal Employment Opportunity Commission better known as the EEOC and law suits as well. Therefore, Executives alike, I am REALLY encouraging you to take a major inventory of what's going on inside of your organizations at the grass roots level so as to address these and other types of issues before you become the poster child for wrongdoings. To be very clear, I'm not advocating for the employee or the employer, what I am suggesting is that good assessments and fair remedies are win-win for any organization as a whole.

Also, get past the facade and realize that employees more and more are understanding authenticity, or what is real and what really makes a difference. To illustrate this point, a friend recalled working for an organization that was really in tuned with employees psychologically and emotionally. Every quarter or three months, executives, managers including my friend would gather with new employees from various departments in a party style room to showcase that choosing to work for that particular organization was a good decision and investment. In addition, the President of that organization invested thousands of dollars into video production in an effort to highlight the organization's achievements as well as its involvement with the community. This video had before and after shots of sick patients, mostly cancer patients and during the entire video, my friend explained that there was an air of melancholy music which gave the feeling that you were in a theater watching a sad movie, you know like when the hero triumphantly saves the earth from destruction or something like that. And it never failed, at a certain point, my friend explained that she would always survey the room to see if anyone were crying, and as usual, it wasn't a dry eye in the entire room. My friend explained that she even had tears in her eyes, and although she had seen the video lots of times, it still played on her psyche.

The trouble with this scenario is that although the organization was a strong leader in the healthcare industry, it didn't support employee engagement or respect employee opinions which deviated from and was contrary to what the video had depicted to new hires. For a very long time, my friend explained that she often felt that it was something morally wrong with this sort of dog and pony show, but keenly understood that even the toughest of moral convictions would never challenge senior leadership. The quote from Harvey Dent, a character in the motion picture "The Dark Knight" when he says, "You're either going to die a hero, or live long enough to become a villain" really captures the essence of my friend's company. In this case, if you work long enough for any organization that condones this type of culture, you could certainly become a villain.

The secret to all of this is to become acutely aware of what's going on around you. I'm not suggesting that you cry wolf every time something happens that you do not agree with, but what I am saying is that you have to read between the metaphorical lines with regards to what is right and wrong. In essence some things are going to be out of your control at different levels in the food chain of power. Nevertheless, you must not stir the pot unless you have a strategic plan in place that will protect you as well as others, because remember the dynamics of any corporation is bigger than any one person. It's not the President of any organization to fully blame for setbacks because he or she is really an institution of thoughts which sometimes leads to dysfunction and that in and of itself is an argument for a different book.

In short, some people are going to say that you are a coward for not speaking up. To a certain degree, they are correct; however, you also have to think about your own well being and that of your family if you have one. Also, the person who thinks that you are a coward most likely has not spoken up for themselves either. Remember, misery loves company, as the old saying goes, so you definitely do not want to fall in with that bunch either. Awareness for the most part, brings energy to the other senses which help you to make better decisions and choices that will guide you in the right direction. Believe me, the answers will come to you and you will certainly move out of an organization that exhibits, encourages and supports dysfunctional or inappropriate behavior.

Consider this, not only is psychological management at your job or in your work, but it's also in your community which creates many of your realities. In many of our states, cities and communities alike, politicians have made it their duty to say that they are changing lives etc. when in fact it's mostly propaganda or commercial appeal. If you don't believe me, just turn on the television and you'll see politicians helping others in the community which plays on the emotions of the individuals watching. The reality is, there are politicians that work really hard and who really care about the conditions of others, but you rarely see these individuals on TV, it's because they are too busy working in the communities away from the media.

## COMMUNICATION IS KEY

My best friend Reginald once told me that the *"height reduces the visibility of what's happening on the floor."* As an Engineer, he was referring to some aspect of an engineering project from work, but this statement to me sort of captures the idea that when you are working in a leadership role, sometimes the reality of what's going on at the staff level may be somewhat cloudy due to other things that you may be involved with. Now, I'm not suggesting that employees turn down promotional opportunities to avoid leadership, but what I am saying is that once in a leadership role, employees should always disseminate as well as receive information openly and strive to fully understand and grasp what's going on at the grass roots or staff level.

The essence of this chapter is denial; however, if asked, most executives at organizations would probably respond with something to this effect, *"We're doing fine"*, *"We're making strides"* or some rendition of both statements. The truth of the matter is that executives are not doing in most cases as well as they claim or think in terms of the social ramifications at the grass roots level. This may be largely in part due to workers fear of retaliation for reporting work related concerns such as issues involving terms and conditions of work to leadership. In a lot of cases, employees are opting to miss work rather than to deal with addressing concerns. To illustrate this point, the Bureau of Labor Statistics, a division of the U.S. Department of Labor reported that in 2011, *"Twenty-one percent of wage and salary workers took paid or unpaid leave during an average week. Worker's who took leave during an average week took an average of 15.6 hours of leave."* One of the main reasons reported to the Bureau was overexertion which accounted for a full quarter of missed workdays across a range of fields.

Overexertion may stem from a number of factors; however, it is very important for leaders to effectively communicate with employees regarding the state of the organization. If you do not communicate such matters openly, you may find that your employees are missing in action, not caring about work or worse, not doing the work. In either case, the organization will take a downward spiral.

Consider this scenario; a friend of mine worked in the Human Resources Department for a major organization that was experiencing some important budget concerns as most organizations do from time to time. These concerns were important because not only did they affect the organization to include layoffs, restructuring and rightsizing; but, it also affected the personal as well as professional lives of many employees from various departments within the organization. For example, the employees who were not laid off had to absorb the additional work from the employees that were laid off. Nevertheless, this caused a great deal of angst and in some cases reports of overexertion and other types of illnesses which resulted in employees missing days from work. Needless to say, with all of these actions, there were a lot of complaints reported to the CEO and to other Executives at the organization. In typical fashion, when contacted, the CEO instructed the COO, who in turn instructed the Sr. Vice Presidents, who in turn instructed the department Directors, who in turn instructed the department Managers, who in turn reported concerns to Human Resources. As you can see, this is a lot of instructing which usually yields no action or, that everyone redirects the issues in a sort of shuffling game which usually end with finger pointing or blame instead of addressing problems.

Communication is not only key, but it is also powerful and in some cases it even saves lives. In this same organization, my friend who worked in the Human Resources Department was the last person in the path of leadership to receive the original complaint reported to the CEO. I'm not suggesting that CEO's alike should investigate concerns, but what I am recommending is that they become involved in certain matters especially when the matter has the potential to alter lives. In this same scenario, one of the employees that were laid off as a result of budget constraints received inaccurate information regarding the specific reasons as to why they were losing their job. As a result, that employee, walked into my friends office alone, pulled out a gun and demanded to see the CEO. Although highly trained and skilled to deal with problems, my friend could not have prepared herself to deal with a real life situation of this magnitude;

however, moments later, she was able to persuade the gunman to put the weapon away and was able to coordinate via speaker phone with the police in the next room, informing them that the situation was deescalated and that the gunman would be surrendering. This situation turned out good for my friend and I'm sure for others at the organization, but extremely bad for the gunman who was a former employee that just wanted someone to communicate with him and to address his concerns. As a result of his actions, the gunman was arrested, spent some time in jail and was reported to have undergone numerous psychological evaluations.

Some years later, I had dinner with my friend who had decided some years earlier that she would change careers due to the constant reminder of that particular day with the gunman. She explained to me that she was more afraid for what would happen to the gunman rather than fearing for her own life. This notion was very peculiar to me since I was always under the impression that we lived in a self preservationist type of world where the general public only cared for the safety and well-being of themselves. My friend continued explaining to me that the gunman really just wanted an explanation from leadership regarding his benefits since no one had effectively communicated with staff regarding the aftermath of the reduction in force. One thing that I learned from this ordeal that was sort of foreshadowing and years later would change my life, is that organizations should really consider having a genuine communication strategy to the general organization when there are life altering circumstances such as mass layoffs, etc. free from the customary fluff couched in notices that are typically required by the Federal Government.

To be clear, I'm not picking on the Government's standards; however, this topic is sensitive in that years later, I found myself in a similar situation when an employee who had recently been fired from a company and I was the Human Resources contact that interfaced with the employee. Just as my friend had deescalated the situation years earlier, now it was my turn to play Psychologist at an attempt to calm an understandably angry employee potentially saving the lives of many including again, those in leadership. For me, this particular employee was rightfully terminated in that he had violated the company's substance abuse policy. However, he just wanted to inquire about any rehabilitation efforts that would assist him with getting his life back on track. However, for days, many leaders at the company gave him the customary run around, explaining that *"they would call him back"*, or that *"they would see what they could do"*, but never returning the former employee's phone call.

Again, there was a lack of communication and as irony would have it; the former employee came to my office and demanded to see the Chief Operating Officer (COO). I felt like I was in the Twilight Zone or some Alfred Hitchcock movie because just as my friend had experienced a similar situation years earlier, I found myself about to go through the same hell. Although this individual didn't have a gun or a weapon, at least he didn't claim to have one, the individual was visibly and physically upset to the point that he was pounding on my desk demanding to speak to the COO. After minutes, which seemed like hours of allowing him to vent, I calmly explained to him that he needed to consider other options, I also explained that he needed to calm down so that I could help him with his concerns because it was my job to do so. I talked him off the metaphorical ledge often referring to the many pictures of my family members throughout my office explaining to him that I couldn't wait to get home to see them. I discussed his family and his children and explained to him that I wanted him to get home safely. Finally, he left without incident and throughout this entire ordeal I had forgotten to push my panic button located under my desk for emergency purposes.

I walked down to the Executive Suite or E-Suite as it was often referred and met with the COO to explain what had just transpired moments before in my office and to my dismay, the COO simply said and I will never forget, *"That guy was a nut case..."*. I walked back to my office sat in my chair and started to cry wondering why the COO didn't at least say thank you, job well done or at least cared enough to tell me to go home for the rest of the day. I was mortified and could not mentally grasp what was happening to the human spirit. I thought to myself, was this COO completely oblivious or just plain ignorant to the fact of what had happened to me and to the organization for that matter. For me, I had saved his life, wow, what a way to thank someone.

Years ago, I would say that these examples would have been extreme to use in a book; however, with all of the tragedies occurring in the world today, these examples are not only relevant, but prevalent. There are many lives lost unnecessarily each year at organizations which in some cases could have been prevented. To mitigate and hopefully eliminate these types of incidents in the workplace, leaders may want to consider talking to employees about the state of the organization, even if the news is bad news, employees tend to be more understanding when executives are honest. I'm not suggesting that employers totally change certain actions such as reductions in forces, rightsizing, etc. based on the personal lives of employees or fear from what could happen; however, what I am suggesting is that positive communication could save lives. The examples above are just two of many scenarios that could end tragically to include injuries and deaths.

Shortly thereafter, I left that company and moved on to dealing with greater tragedies in other organizations only to realize that organizations alike all have similar problems and that if not dealt with properly, that meant I could be running from organization to organization my entire career. Again, bad or ineffective systems need to change, not employees.

## Complete Denial

I must say that for years I was mad at that COO for not taking the time to see if I was okay, for not fully understanding the dynamics of my near death experience and for his complete disregard for the human spirit. However, through my experiences working for several organizations in various industries, I am glad to report that I had ups and downs and crazy experiences. Most importantly, had it not been for those experiences personally and that of my colleagues, I would not have been able to disseminate the information in this book. When I look back on my experiences working for various organizations, it's sort of comical and that too has helped me throughout the years in dealing with the denial that often exists in many organizations.

To help illustrate this point, I came across the following allegory by accident, *Story of the Emperor's New Clothes* by Hans Christian Andersen while perusing the public domain on-line. When I read this story, I had mixed emotions of laughter and anger because it reminded me of what I personally experienced in my plight of trying to explain certain realities that occurred at organizations only to be informed that *"We're doing okay as an organization."* I remember thinking that this story would be a great reference in a book to show the comedic side of what often happens when employees and leaders are in denial at organizations. Please read the following allegory carefully for its humor, but more importantly, for its real message:

> Many years ago there lived an Emperor who was so fond of new clothes that he spent all his money on them in order to be beautifully dressed. He did not care about his soldiers, he did not care about the theatre; he only liked to go out walking to show off his new clothes. He had a coat for every hour of the day; and just as they say of a king, 'He is

in the council-chamber,' they always said here, 'The Emperor is in the wardrobe.'

In the great city in which he lived there was always something going on; every day many strangers came there. One day two impostors arrived who gave themselves out as weavers, and said that they knew how to manufacture the most beautiful cloth imaginable. Not only were the texture and pattern uncommonly beautiful, but the clothes which were made of the stuff possessed this wonderful property that they were invisible to anyone who was not fit for his office, or who was unpardonably stupid.

'Those must indeed be splendid clothes,' thought the Emperor. 'If I had them on I could find out which men in my kingdom are unfit for the offices they hold; I could distinguish the wise from the stupid! Yes, this cloth must be woven for me at once.' And he gave both the impostors much money, so that they might begin their work.

They placed two weaving-looms, and began to do as if they were working, but they had not the least thing on the looms. They also demanded the finest silk and the best gold, which they put in their pockets, and worked at the empty looms till late into the night.

'I should like very much to know how far they have got on with the cloth,' thought the Emperor. But he remembered when he thought about it that whoever was stupid or not fit for is office would not be able to see it. Now he certainly believed that he had nothing to fear for himself, but he wanted first to send somebody else in order to see how he stood with regard to his office. Everybody in the whole town knew what a wonderful power the cloth had, and they were all curious to see how bad or how stupid their neighbor was.

'I will send my old and honored minister to the weavers,' thought the Emperor. 'He can judge best what the cloth is like, for he has intellect, and no one understands his office better than he.'

Now the good old minister went into the hall where the two impostors sat working at the empty weaving-looms. 'Dear me!' thought the old minister, opening his eyes wide, 'I can see nothing!' But he did not say so.

Both the impostors begged him to be so kind as to step closer, and asked him if it were not a beautiful texture and lovely colors. They pointed to the empty loom, and the poor old minister went forward rubbing his eyes; but he could see nothing, for there was nothing there.

'Dear, dear!' thought he, 'can I be stupid? I have never thought that, and nobody must know it! Can I be not fit for my office? No, I must certainly not say that I cannot see the cloth!'

'Have you nothing to say about it?' asked one of the men who was weaving.

'Oh, it is lovely, most lovely!' answered the old minister, looking through his spectacles. 'What a texture! What colors! Yes, I will tell the Emperor that it pleases me very much.'

'Now we are delighted at that,' said both the weavers, and thereupon they named the colors and explained the make of the texture.

The old minister paid great attention, so that he could tell the same to the Emperor when he came back to him, which he did.

The impostors now wanted more money, more silk, and more gold to use in their weaving. They put it all in their own pockets, and there came no threads on the loom, but they went on as they had done before, working at the empty loom. The Emperor soon sent another worthy statesman to see how the weaving was getting on, and whether the cloth would soon be finished. It was the same with him as the first one; he looked and looked, but because there was nothing on the empty loom he could see nothing.

'Is it not a beautiful piece of cloth?' asked the two impostors, and they pointed to and described the splendid material which was not there.

'Stupid I am not!' thought the man, 'so it must be my good office for which I am not fitted. It is strange, certainly, but no one must be allowed to notice it.' And so he praised the cloth which he did not see, and expressed to them his delight at the beautiful colors and the splendid texture. 'Yes, it is quite beautiful,' he said to the Emperor.

Everybody in the town was talking of the magnificent cloth.

Now the Emperor wanted to see it himself while it was still on the loom. With a great crowd of select followers, amongst whom were both the worthy statesmen who had already been there before, he went to the cunning impostors, who were now weaving with all their might, but without fiber or thread.

'Is it not splendid!' said both the old statesmen who had already been there. 'See, your Majesty, what a texture! What colors?' And then they pointed to the empty loom, for they believed that the others could see the cloth quite well.

'What!' thought the Emperor, 'I can see nothing? This is indeed horrible! Am I stupid? Am I not fit to be Emperor? That was the most dreadful thing that could happen to me. Oh, it is very beautiful,' he said. 'It has my gracious approval.' And then he nodded pleasantly, and examined the empty loom, for he would not say that he could see nothing.

His whole Court round him looked and looked, and saw no more than the others; but they said like the Emperor, 'Oh! It is beautiful!' And they advised him to wear these new and magnificent clothes for the first time at the great procession which was soon to take place. 'Splendid! Lovely! Most beautiful!' went from mouth to mouth; everyone seemed delighted over them, and the Emperor gave to the impostors the title of Court weavers to the Emperor.

Throughout the whole of the night before the morning on which the procession was to take place, the impostors were up and were working by the light of over sixteen candles. The people could see that they were very busy making the Emperor's new clothes ready. They pretended they were taking the cloth from the loom, cut with huge scissors in the air, sewed with needles without thread, and then said at last, 'Now the clothes are finished!'

The Emperor came himself with his most distinguished knights, and each impostor held up his arm just as if he were holding something, and said, 'See! Here are the breeches! Here is the coat! Here the cloak!' and so on.

'Spun clothes are so comfortable that one would imagine one had nothing on at all; but that is the beauty of it!'

'Yes,' said all the knights, but they could see nothing, for there was nothing there.

'Will it please your Majesty graciously to take off your clothes,' said the impostors, 'then we will put on the new clothes, here before the mirror.'

The Emperor took off all his clothes, and the impostors placed themselves before him as if they were putting on each part of his new clothes which was ready, and the Emperor turned and bent himself in front of the mirror.

'How beautifully they fit! How well they sit!' said everybody? 'What material! What colors! It is a gorgeous suit!'

'They are waiting outside with the canopy which your Majesty is wont to have borne over you in the procession,' announced the Master of the Ceremonies.

'Look, I am ready,' said the Emperor. 'Doesn't it sit well?' And he turned himself again to the mirror to see if his finery was on all right.

The chamberlains who were used to carry the train put their hands near the floor as if they were lifting up the train; then they did as if they were holding something in the air. They would not have it noticed that they could see nothing.

So the Emperor went along in the procession under the splendid canopy, and all the people in the streets and at the windows said, 'How matchless are the Emperor's new clothes! That train fastened to his dress, how beautifully it hangs!'

No one wished it to be noticed that he could see nothing, for then he would have been unfit for his office, or else very stupid. None of the Emperor's clothes had met with such approval as these had.

'But he has nothing on!' said a little child at last.

'Just listen to the innocent child!' said the father, and each one whispered to his neighbor what the child had said.

'But he has nothing on!' the whole of the people called out at last.

This struck the Emperor, for it seemed to him as if they were right; but he thought to himself, 'I must go on with the procession now. And the chamberlains walked along still more uprightly, holding up the train which was not there at all.

If you're like me, I'm sure that you can identify with this story and you're probably laughing your socks off at the correlation of what often happens within the ranks at your organization. This story was written many years ago; although comical, its content is very applicable to what's occurring now. Denial is something very serious and can cause situations to be fatal at work if not properly addressed. Like me, you may want to consider opting to work for another company if the denial is too overwhelming within your current organization. Remember, your health and wellbeing comes first and foremost.

*"One wanders to the left, another to the right. Both are equally in error, but, are seduced by different delusions."*

~ HORACE

# CHAPTER 4

# DEALING WITH POLITICAL REALITIES IN THE WORKPLACE

IN ORDER TO DEAL WITH political realities, you must first understand what they are. This chapter will discuss the nature and circumstances of political realities in the workplace, and more importantly, how to navigate through and deal with them. If you ask your colleagues about politics in the workplace chances are you may receive a plethora of answers and examples. I want to be very clear about something; political realities exist and are very real despite what some might say about the subject. The reason why this subject is somewhat ambiguous to some is because many who experience politics in the workplace are not even aware that it's happening or that they are being governed by it.

To understand political realities in the workplace, one must first ask the questions, is there reality in politics? Do politicians seem genuine to you? Are they looking out for your best interests? The same holds for executives in organizations and companies alike. Let's be fair, although there are genuine leaders in organizations who really want nothing more than to do the right things with regards to the treatment of their employees; however, there are certain political realities that often preclude this from happening. Put another way let's define reality or what is real. According to philosophy, *reality is the state of things as they actually exist, rather than as they may appear or might be imagined. In a wider definition, reality includes everything that is and has been, whether or not it is observable or comprehensible.* Therefore, there are certain political dealings that occur within organizations that hold as truths rather than what's actually happening.

I came across an essay called *Political Realities* by S. Leon Felkins while perusing the internet and thought it was a terrific description of what often happens in the workplace. Now, some might argue that the context of this material is irrelevant or that the description is wrong; however, unless you are working on the planet Mars everyday; political realities are prevalent within the confines of every job in every industry:

> "To be governed is to be watched, inspected, spied upon, directed, law-driven, numbered, regulated, enrolled, indoctrinated, preached at, controlled, checked, estimated, valued, censured, commanded, by creatures who have neither the right nor the wisdom nor the virtue to do so. To be governed is to be at every operation, at every transaction, noted, registered, counted, taxed, stamped, measured, numbered, assessed, licensed, authorized, admonished, prevented, forbidden, reformed, corrected, punished. It is, under pretext of public

utility, and in the name of the general interest, to be placed under contribution, drilled, fleeced, exploited, monopolized, extorted from, squeezed, hoaxed, robbed; then, at the slightest resistance, the first word of complaint, to be repressed, fined, vilified, harassed, hunted down, abused, clubbed, disarmed, sacrificed, sold, betrayed, and to crown all, mocked, ridiculed, derided, outraged, dishonored. That is government; that is its justice; that is its morality."

For the record, I do not want anyone to misinterpret the message above. I am not talking about nor am I referring to the Federal Government of the United States; I'm merely attempting to use the above quote as a metaphor to describe certain politics that often exist in the workplace and how employees have purported to experience them. If you will notice in the passage, the terms are action oriented in that they suggest some form of behavior taken by an entity against another entity. As an employee, you may have at some point in your career experienced some form of at least one or more of the actions in the passage above as the recipient or worst, as the donor.

In an organization, there are typically three types of employees: One, an employee that is part of what happens in an organization. I refer to this type of employee as a Freelancer; beware of these individuals, as they are those who are self-promoting and go about day to day doing whatever they have to do at work to get ahead, even if it means stepping on someone's neck in the process. This employee is for the most part acutely active in the goings on within organizations, even if it's at the cost of doing something wrong; typically, this employee will not rock the boat and/or speak up against something for which he or she knows is inappropriate or unfair; and is often loyal to themselves and not the organization for which they bolster to be.

For example, a friend of mine inquired of my advice on a situation that occurred at her job and wanted to know how or if she should intervene with the CEO. It seemed that an executive at the organization in which she worked had a habit of encouraging those in management to hire friends, acquaintances, associates and friends of associates of the CEO, Board Members and other entities at her organization. Even if the CEO met someone at a golfing event while standing in the refreshment line, management was encouraged to give them an interview. My friend worked in the organization's Human Resources Department in the Recruiting and Talent Acquisition Office and her duties not only entailed recruiting candidates to work for the organization; but also, she had the responsibility of ensuring that candidates were recruited fairly. Due to the fact that certain managers were just trying to please the CEO by hiring his buddies, friends and friends of friends, this practice made it very difficult for my friend to conduct operations fairly.

Now, on the surface, this seemed like a very fair practice considering that everyone wants to please the CEO right? Another major problem, besides the obvious is that what type of message is CEO's that encourage this type of behavior really sending out to their organizations. Remember, CEO's alike, set the tone for the organization and typically others follow suit or ultimately may have to look for another job. Make no mistake about it, this particular CEO was very aware of what was going on in terms of who was getting hired. Also, let's face it, a CEO will never admit to saying that he or she has emphatically told anyone within their organization that they are required to hire someone regardless of the rules, etc. However, if you've been in the business world especially corporate, as long as I have, as an employee, you are acutely aware of the signals and corporate ease in directing you to do something regardless of how it's communicated. The lesson here is to learn how to navigate through the system without taking things personally, because remember, you're really not in control and sending the wrong signals could stunt your career growth.

My friend explained that while conducting an audit of employees that worked at her firm, she noticed that several of those employees in leadership roles were not qualified to do the jobs at the time that they were hired. Also, it appeared that several executives at her organization had hired friends that they had worked with at previous jobs, not taking their qualifications into account. Talk about nepotism, my friend even informed me that her colleagues were known to do almost anything in which the CEO wanted or requested, even if it meant bending or breaking the rules in an effort to please the CEO. Nevertheless, I informed my friend to be very careful with regards to her actions and to consider what was really at stake to include her family, finances and well-being.

To some, I know that you may think that this advice to my friend may have been unorthodox; however, when dealing with political realities at work, *and you will*, sometimes you have to tolerate inappropriate behaviors until you can move out of that type of environment. Remember, the best experience in life comes from experience itself. I have been confronted by many situations where I've had to make critical decisions based on office politics, control, manipulation and a host of other unpleasant situations. Nevertheless, I too had to think about my personal situation until I could move as soon as possible out of those organizations that condoned such behavior. Responding to political realities differently; may get you in trouble with management, put you on their radar to be watched or worst, terminated.

The second type of employee is one that watches things happen at an organization. I refer to this type of employee as the Watcher. Watchers are the opposite of Freelancers in that they are typically loyal to an organization. Watchers for the most part are quiet and it can be a challenge sometimes to determine where they stand on certain issues. The Watcher is truly a mid-point person in that they can easily become a member of the Freelancer Group as well as the Oblivion

Group which is the third type of employee. For example, Watchers are often aware of the wrongdoings within organizations but will not rock the boat so as to maintain their neutrality stance on issues, thereby removing themselves from Management's metaphorical radar. In essence, by reframing from making complaints or challenging the status quo, the Watcher then assumes some of the Oblivion characteristics in that they become a non-threat to the organization unless they feel themselves threatened.

On the flip side of things, the Freelancer and the Watcher can and sometimes will turn against the organization and in some cases have the ability to bring down the house with complaints, lawsuits, EEOC charges, you name it, considering that they know most of the dirty dealings that happen within organizations. Of note, Freelancers and Watchers can be in leadership roles or staff roles this is why they can be so detrimental to organizations.

To illustrate this point, while having dinner one night, a colleague of mine told me a story that I found to be very useful in describing Freelancers and Watchers. It seems that one of the Managers at his organization, who was also a friend, was terminated and as a result decided to fire back at the organization shortly after being terminated. My friend explained that this particular employee was very loyal to the organization in his many years of service and very diligent in his rise to management. Now, this would seem like everyone's goal of rising to the top at any organization, without being terminated of course.

The Good Part! This manager was terminated due to missing a lot of days from work as a result of an illness. I know what you're thinking, that's not legal, is it? In some cases it's not; however, the reality is, this employee was terminated. The organization's stance was that the employee was a member of management and they couldn't afford to have someone in a critical needs position out all of the time. In some cases the organization's position was perfectly acceptable;

however, in this case, they messed with the wrong employee. Not only did he fire back, but he did so with a vengeance.

As a Freelancer, he did everything for the Executives, including assisting them with burying their wrongdoings throughout the years. As a Watcher, he avoided speaking out against the wrongdoings, but the caveat and nail in the coffin sort to speak was a journal in which the employee kept detailing and implicating every wrongdoing and executive that was involved for nearly a decade. I mean there were wrongful terminations, discriminations, bribery, you name it. And yes, you know where all of this was headed, that's right, court. My friend explained to me that this case was the shortest case and settlement in the history of lawsuits. This particular manager, walked away with nearly a million dollars for defamation, discrimination and the kitchen sink. Also, a Governmental Agency became involved in the case and slapped all sorts of fines on this organization.

The third and final type of employee is the one who asks what happened at an organization. I refer to this type of employee as the Oblivion because they are for the most part, unaware of the political realities that are often prevalent within the organization. Oblivions are typically loyal to organizations because it feels right to them; they come to work every day but truly are from Mars. Although oblivions, this type of employee can be very dangerous to the general workforce population in that they believe everything that is said without question; even if the information presented is substantiated to be overwhelmingly inaccurate.

To illustrate the behavior of this type of employee, I have to go back to my earlier days as an under graduate student in college. I was twenty-one years old and very green (*i.e., new to most things*); however, due to my upbringing, I was very keen on my surroundings. I was working at a Department Store in downtown Houston. The reason why I'm giving the location is because this particular store is a landmark and has a lot of history with regards to the community and social changes. Anyway, while in college I became the manager of the Paint Department. This was a great experience for me and would be the beginning of shaping what would come later in my life.

While working at this store, I worked with a guy named Randy who was Asian American and a consummate Oblivion that believed everything sputtered out of the mouths of management as well as staff members. One day, a store manager was transferred, not fired, for making negative and inappropriate comments about Asian Americans. As luck would have it, one of my colleagues was a witness to the accusations brought against the store manager. I felt really bad and upset that a human being would say something disparaging about another human being because of the difference in race. I mean, I was so upset you would have thought that I was leading a protest or something. However, when I discussed the situation with Randy and explained that it was unbelievable that the company did not fire the store manager. Randy simply explained that he couldn't believe that the company transferred the manager, because only one witness said that he made the inappropriate comment and how could anyone prove that the manager had made the comment. Later, it was revealed that this same manager was alleged to have made similar comments about another ethnic minority group at another store prior to becoming the manager of our store.

I couldn't believe my ears; Randy was actually defending the person who had made racist comments against him with such optimism, I felt as though I was trapped in the story called *Candide* by Voltaire, you know, the story of the sheltered optimist who is forced from his sheltered life and ventures into the world. Just like Candide, Randy's plight of ignorance and naivety reflected in that *"everything is for the best in this best of all possible worlds."* Poor guy, in the end, I actually felt sorry for them, both Candide and Randy. There were many days afterwards that I was mad and confused at the sheer disrespect and even more angry at people like Randy who refused to acknowledge that wrongdoings were happening within the organization. I didn't know whether to choke Randy or the members of management. The good thing which kept me going was the fact that I was very close to completing my college degree which meant that I would not be working with Randy or that particular organization much longer.

Where do you fit in the scheme of things? You may want to think about the people in your organization and assess their characteristics and how they compare to that of Freelancers, Watchers or Oblivions. This is comical in some ways, but very real in the sense that this is actually happening in every organization whether you want to admit it or not. A friend of mine once told me after hearing me complain about my personal problems that I needed to take off my metaphorical goggles that were blocking my ability to see things clearly. What my friend was referring to made perfect sense, because all of us from time to time refuse to see things for what they really are because we are often times scared to make the necessary adjustments, sometimes this means moving onto a better situation.

## MANAGEMENT IS AN INSTITUTION

The Office of the President of the United States is an institution and not one person, the same holds for companies and organizations. Just as the President of the United States has a cabinet comprised of individuals with specific job functions, an organization's Chief Executive Officer or CEO typically has a cabinet or staff of Executives with specific functions. Although there's usually one person at the helm, in either case he or she is rarely pushing the organization's agenda alone. The CEO is the leading executive officer of a corporation charged with principal responsibility of the organization and accountable to the owners, board of directors, stockholders, etc. The CEO's basic function is to provide overall leadership to the organization by establishing direction, overseeing senior executives, and to function as the organization's primary contact for outside entities. The emergence of the CEO is in close correlation to the growth of industry. As organizations became too large and complex for any one individual to operate, other executives emerged to assist CEO's with operations. In fact, the cumulative responsibilities of CEO's have become so complex that many organizations have established segments within the company in which responsibilities are divided among high level executives.

In establishing direction for the organization, the CEO typically sets crucial objectives and annual goals to steer the organization's business. In some cases the CEO may seek guidance and approval from a governing board to set goals and objectives, the CEO is ultimately responsible for the overall direction of the organization. To help with achieving goals and objectives, typically the CEO will formulate strategies and get the buy in from members of his cabinet or executive team so that messages are on the same accord when disseminated to the general workforce.

As the primary person for overseeing senior executives, the CEO often has the daunting task of developing executives, maintaining organizational structure and the responsibility for all decisions that will potentially affect the organization's well-being. In creating organizational structure, the CEO depends heavily on members of his or her executive team to carry out major functions to each of the organization's segments, as well as provide accountability among these segments.

Finally, the CEO is the primary contact for outside entities to include being the decision maker with regards to addressing decisions that can impact the organization. What does all of this mean for you as an employee? With much responsibility of keeping the organization's budget intact, the many board meetings to discuss and assess the state of the organization, overseeing executive leaders and a host of other duties, it is understandable that most CEO's will likely be unfamiliar with what happens in the lower levels with regards to the day to day personnel issues within an organization.

Now, this is not to say that all CEO's alike are totally unaware of what happens at the bottom rungs of the organization's ladder of employment or that they are bad people; personally, I know several CEO's and they are very good people, they are just out of touch with reality; however, even with some awareness of issues, they are still much too busy to adequately address concerns. Having said that, the next time that you find yourself in a situation that warrants some form of complaint, you may want to consider the executive players and how they are aligned to the chief shot caller. Remember, one of the CEO's top priorities is to mitigate or eliminate potential impact to the organization. So unless you have something that will bring the company to its knees sort to speak, I would highly encourage you to find another avenue to get your message across.

This is not to allow someone or something to walk all over you to include discrimination, harassment, inappropriate behavior, etc. However, I'm merely trying to get you in the mindset of the bigger picture and how organizations alike operate as an institution and not a single entity. Nevertheless, I encourage you to navigate with caution and to always be very smart about your moves through the organization as though you were in a giant chess game.

## Don't Kick the Culture

I took a job in the healthcare industry because I was so amazed at the type of work that the employees were doing, I mean the hair still literally stand up on the back of my neck when I see a life flight helicopter in the air because I know that a patient is in good hands going to the Texas Medical Center in Houston, TX. The Medical Center has an amazing array of talented and gifted professionals of who I am very proud and honored to say that I work with. However, just as with any good thing there is a very bad side to the equation. In this segment I will discuss the benefits of being positive even in the midst of craziness.

There is a certain culture or behavior, belief and characteristic of a particular group that guides an organization and even if you do not agree with and/or understand the culture, one major benefit to your survival at any organization is to never engage in making or agreeing with negative comments about the organization especially in conversations with others. As the old adage goes, we live in a very small world and the whole world is listening whether you believe this or not, it may lead to your demise. As I've mentioned before, I work in Employee Relations, so I'm often meeting with employees to discuss concerns and to find solutions to problems. While meeting with employees I sometimes hear them complain about being harassed and gossiping about management and how bad they feel the organization is as a whole. In some cases, I often wonder who in their right mind would want to work at a place that allows and encourages this much chaos. People literally sit in my office for hours sometimes to the point that they are in tears and in fear for their lives, I ask you does any of this sound familiar to you? I'm sometimes amazed at the stories that are reported to me, what's more amazing is the fact that most executives are sometimes already aware of the complaints before I can even talk about what's happening in a particular area of the organization.

Also, there's another old adage that says, pick your battles carefully. Sometimes I'm often summoned to the executive suite to discuss personnel issues that have potential impacts to the organization. What I've learned in these meetings is that executives have metaphorical radars with a list of who they deem as trouble makers, even if the complaining employee has merit to their complaint, for the most part, they are still viewed as troublesome. Again, I'm not suggesting that you keep all concerns to yourself, because the reality is that some concerns warrant intervention from the organization. However, have you ever pondered how executives might have knowledge of a concern that you haven't even shared with anyone? Again, we live in a very small world and you must safeguard carefully the things that you share with others. In my mother's kitchen, there's a plaque on the wall with a picture of a knife and fork and a passage that reads:

> As you go through life brother,
> Keep your words short and sweet,
> Because you never know from time to time,
> Which ones you'll have to eat.

I've read this plaque hundreds of times even as a kid growing up and it finally makes sense to me and is very useful in my day to day work. Also, I often use it to inspire employees that visit my office complaining about others within the organization.

There's another old saying that I'm sure everyone is familiar with, "The grass always seems greener on the other side", this is especially true for people who because of angst are in a hurry to leave their current job to work at another organization. The only problem with this is that in most companies and organizations, you will find much of the same problems and concerns. Think of it this way, can you recall when you first started a new job; I'll bet the organization was probably presented to you as *"One of the best places to work"*. Also, you probably saw this same quote in Newsweek or some other well known periodical claiming that the organization is the leader in this or that. These statistics for the most part are true; however, we're talking about the organization's behavior which for the most part is not in those statistics. Let's face it; most organizations are experiencing similar concerns and are becoming more and more inclined to avoid dealing with them.

Another important concept in understanding culture is to avoid backstabbing which is defined by Merriam-Webster as *"betrayal as by a verbal attack against one not present especially by a false friend."* To illustrate this concept, years ago while attending an important organizational function, I was working my way around the room during the meet and greet portion of the function which also entailed drinking alcoholic cocktails and eating light appetizers. Needless to say whenever there's alcoholic beverages being consumed, employees tend to engage in tell all rants which can become very annoying. Anyway, as I was making my way around the room, I ran into an up and coming executive who immediately jumped into a backstabbing session. He complained about everyone in the leadership chain including the CEO. If anyone listening were to believe his raving including myself would have wondered how on earth anyone could work for such a screwed up company. After all, everyone in the leadership chain was stupid except of course, for him. The crazy part about this conversation with this executive is that I don't even think that he realized the impression that he was making. Apparently, backstabbing was part of his modus operandi.

The scary part about this conversation is that this type of person is not alone in exhibiting this type of behavior. As an Employee Relations Professional, I'm often in attendance at numerous corporate functions and have the pleasure of listening to employees regardless of their position within the organization, complain about everyone from the janitor on up to the CEO. Another thing that I've learned is that people who continue to backstab others do so because they lack personal confidence and are genuinely scared about what others think about them. Also, to a certain extent, no one has informed them that backstabbing is wrong and that it makes them appear untrustworthy. Just as a child who's disrespectful to his elders; often continues to engage in such disrespectful behavior due to the fact that there are no consequences for the inappropriate behavior. The same holds for someone who backstabs, they will stop engaging in this type of behavior when there are consequences.

Consider this, the executive above that annoyed me for several minutes which seemed like hours, would probably never have talked openly about the employees the way in which he spoke about them to me. I'm sure that he would have laughed in their faces while continuing to talk about them behind their backs and I'm most certain that he would not have addressed the President of the organization in the same manner that he described to me. The irony of all of this is that this individual was receiving the President's Award for Distinction all while talking about the President in a very bad way.

One important note, remember when I said how do you think information gets back to people, well it's not just complaints that gets back to executives; also, people who gossip tend to think that just because someone listening may agree with them from time to time that they are speaking to someone safe. Wrong! It is almost predestined that when you backstab someone, the people who you are sharing the information with don't trust you as well. Think about it this way, most of the people you are sharing information with work for the same company that you do and even if the person that you are sharing gossip with is backstabbing others as well by engaging in the conversation, there's a remote chance that they will talk about you behind your back as well.

All of this creates a never ending cycle which diminishes or eradicates trust. Now, I'm not saying that I've never participated or been the person engaging in backstabbing another; however, as with everything, experience is the greatest teacher and I have learned that backstabbing is not only a risky business but it is a cowardly way of communicating. One good benefit to understanding culture is to stop backstabbing and complaining all together.

## GET CONNECTED

---

To fully understand your organization and how it works, you must become aware of its history, mission and have the ability to build relationships even if you don't agree with certain things that happen at the organization, having this insight will put you ahead of the herd. The workplace has always primarily been about who you know and not about what you know as the old adage goes. Now, I know what some of you may be thinking, you are really not the type to kiss up to people. And you are absolutely correct. This segment is not about teaching you how to become a sycophant, but rather how having a positive relationship can assist your career without you losing your identity. Nevertheless, don't let anyone fool you; rising to the top in any organization requires being connected to others who are already connected.

Relationships are very important in organizations and have been so for many years; even before the gigantic boom of technology people relied heavily upon the relationships of others. Unlike backstabbing, relationship building is an art and requires knowledge, wisdom and integrity. Remember, knowledge and wisdom comes from studying the organization's history and familiarizing yourself with key players. Leaders in general feel comfortable and are generally impressed when you are able to disseminate information about their organization in a positive and professional manner, even if you don't agree with it. In addition, your wisdom establishes credibility and makes the recipient feel relaxed around you. Also, integrity speaks volumes to others about your character and it is a very crucial ingredient to have.

Think of it this way, have you ever gone into a department store to purchase something only to have a representative of the store to treat you unprofessionally, not a good feeling is it? The reverse is when you experience superior service; it makes you feel as though you are the only customer in the store, especially when the representative is knowledgeable about the product in which you are purchasing, what an incredible feeling.

If you take the time to discipline yourself and work at establishing relationships with people in the know, I promise you that a whole world of opportunities will open up for you. In addition, you will stand out from the pack and will be more effective when dealing with others. To illustrate this point, my wife's boss also a director at her firm was once the secretary for the firm's CEO. However, because my wife's boss had the desire and passion to develop positive relationships, she not only moved up the ladder rather quickly, but most recently, one of the firms executives left the organization and the President was looking for a replacement, guess who got the job? That's correct, my wife's boss.

Of note, during the time that my wife's current boss was the CEO's secretary, I forgot to mention that this same CEO was stricken with cancer, and my wife' boss took care of the CEO beyond her administrative duties at work, it became personal to include picking up the CEO's son from school, grocery shopping, doing laundry to the point of being the CEO's personal help. Now, some of you may say that this type of behavior from a former secretary, now member of the executive team, was the epitome of butt kissing; however, this relationship catapulted her career from administrative duties to executive level duties. Having said that, I'm not suggesting that you run out and start picking up your boss's children from school, as this might surely get you a meeting with your organization's Employee Assistance Program or some other form of psychological counseling. However, what I am suggesting is that you develop meaningful relationships that will help advance your career.

## Have a Moral Compass

As discussed earlier, political realities are alive in the workplace and are everywhere and they inflict every organization. In fact, you would be hard pressed to find an executive or employee in any organization that has completely avoided the fray. However, although it is very important for you to understand political realities, it's more important for you to have a moral compass or anything which serves to guide a person's decisions based on morals or virtues.

When presented with tough decisions at work, you must always ask yourself, am I doing this to please my boss? Is it in line with my values? What will the outcome render? Also, when contemplating or joining an organization, make sure that the organization's mission and goals are in alignment with your values to include ethics, or whatever is of importance to you. Your decision to work for an organization should never lie within the organization's notoriety. For example, if an organization is the leader in producing a certain item, I'm sure that's not the only driving force that make's a person want to work for that organization. What about things such as character, morals, and other things that seem to be ideals from the past, besides the obvious of course, money.

During an interview with a perspective organization, you can find out a lot of things about the organization by asking questions about the organization's culture. However, keep in mind that there are no guarantees that the information that you are seeking from a representative of an organization in a few hours will sum up the complete picture of the organization's culture in a nutshell. However, with the limited information you have, you may want to seek out other ways in deciding if that organization is a good fit for you. Remember, it's just an interview, and if you do not feel that a certain organization is a good fit then I would suggest that you not accept the position or assignment. Much too often people allow their financial circumstances to dictate what positions they will accept without thinking about the dangers associated with working at a certain organization.

For example, if you accept a position at an organization for which you know condones or encourages certain behaviors; then what does that say about who you really are. In essence, you could be setting yourself up for stress, anxiety and other negative implications. Life is much too short to work for a bad company, wouldn't it be easier to work for a company that does more good than bad. I'll be the first to admit that all companies bear some things that are not so good to talk about; however, it's always been easier to work for a company that does what's right and not what's easy.

*"We are all faced with a series of great opportunities brilliantly disguised as insoluble problems."*

~ JOHN W. GARDNER

# CHAPTER 5

# MAKE AN ADJUSTMENT

In 2005, HURRICANE KATRINA, THE costliest hurricane in U.S. History estimated at $108 billion in damages, ravaged the Gulf Coast area from Louisiana to Florida. Imagine for a moment, that as a result of a hurricane, you lose everything that you own, your home, cars, pictures, family heirlooms, memories, etc. What would you do? This book is entitled Asleep at Work, well let me tell you, to a lot of Gulf Coast residents, Hurricane Katrina was a nightmare of sorts. At the time that Katrina hit the Gulf Coast, I was working for an Agency that was very involved with community efforts in Houston. This was another turning point in my life because it made me realize that I should never take anything for granted including my job, because it could be taken away at a moment's notice.

During the aftermath of Katrina, many people, especially residents of New Orleans, moved to Houston, some temporarily and some permanently. Due to the fact that their move was at a moment's notice, many people had to move into the George R. Brown Convention Center because hotels, motels and other venues were completely booked. However, in the spirit of helping our neighbors to the east, the City of Houston embraced those affected by Katrina supplying shelter, food, medical attention and a host of other services.

The turning point in my life came when the Agency that I worked for volunteered as did a lot of organizations in the Houston and surrounding areas in an effort to provide resources to those affected by Hurricane Katrina. There were thousands of people, some who had just witnessed their entire lives literally washed away; this really affected me to the core especially seeing elderly people and young infants sleeping on cots and other makeshift beddings. While assisting with providing resources, I also had the privilege of speaking to many individuals providing words of encouragement and discussing what was to become in the next chapters in their lives.

I was truly amazed by some of the comments from people that I conversed with, it was as if some had already planned their lives around the aftermath of Katrina. Although there were obvious discussions about the physical things that were removed from some of their lives, the psychological tolls were enormous and in some instances, more devastating than the physical tolls because even though homes, cars and other material things could be replaced, I knew that the way things were before, would be changed forever. Some people would not, as others could not, return to New Orleans which meant that adjustments had to be made in their lives.

Several years after Katrina hit the Gulf Coast, I often met many survivors from New Orleans throughout the city from time to time who now resided in Houston and was amazed at their resiliency and the adjustments they made. When discussing their progress, it felt like Katrina never affected their lives due to their strong faith, belief and plans which ultimately led them to moving on. This enormous courage reminds me of the imaginary character *Haw* from the book *Who Moved My Cheese?* by Spencer Johnson in that making adjustments finding their way and settling in Houston was an enormous journey just as the character Haw learned how to adapt to change in the maze of uncertainty as described in the book, what an amazing story by Spencer Johnson and if you haven't read this book, I highly encourage you to go out and purchase it today as it is very insightful as it expresses how to deal with change in your work and in your life. In comparison to the story *Who Moved My Cheese*, Hurricane Katrina was the Maze of uncertainty for most New Orleans at that time, and their cheese was the life they had prior to the destruction or change by Katrina.

These next segments will focus on how to recover from setbacks in the workplace:

## RECOVER QUICKLY

There are many people that have wronged me over the years and the pain and humiliation that I had to endure at times was unbearable. Years ago, I was asked to resign by the Chief Operating Officer at an organization in which I help to establish the department in which I worked. In personnel terms, being asked to resign is a fancy way of being terminated. If asked, most people would probably express that it wasn't their fault as a result of being terminated. Well, I'm definitely in that crowd. For me, I was asked by the Chief Operating Officer or COO as he was often referred, to develop a plan to recruit and attract applicants with better qualifications to work for the organization. I was up for the task; the only problem with this was that my area of expertise resided in employee relations and not recruitment.

However, when you are asked by a member of the executive team to do something, it's very difficult to explain limitations especially if you're working for an organization that doesn't encourage suggestions or feedback from staff.

At that time, the organization did not have a recruiting office and relied heavily on departmental leadership to recruit candidates for their respective areas of responsibility. The major problem with this was that leaders were not qualified and often discriminated unintentionally when making decisions to hire applicants. As a result of these misfortunes, instead of developing a recruiting department with qualified staff as I had often suggested, the Chief Executive Officer or CEO of the organization felt that my department should take on those additional full time duties of recruiting applicants.

Nevertheless, with limited experience and equally limited time, my staff and I researched best practices, reached out to colleagues from other organizations regarding establishing a recruitment office and to our surprise; we developed a strategic recruitment plan that was very successful and well received by members from middle management up to executive staff. The recruitment plan incorporated members from leadership to serve on an interview panel alongside members from my Employee Relations staff to interview applicants thereby giving a sort of 360 degree feel to the interview process which entailed strategic and analytical feedback. I even gave the recruitment plan a fancy name to solidify the deal and to make the strategy official; the name was the *Talent Search Committee*. Although this was a very daunting task considering the limited time in which we had to pull it all together; the project was very successful, or so we thought.

About a week or so after completing the project, I was summoned to my boss's office for a meeting. When I arrived to her office, the COO was sitting at the table next to her and I remember thinking that perhaps congratulations were in order for having completed the recruitment project. However, to my surprise, I'll never forget the COO's words, as he looked at me and smiled and said *"Shawn, your services are no longer needed"*, as you can imagine, I thought that this was some sort of sick joke. I paused and looked at my boss and then over to the COO and asked what had happened and the COO explained that the CEO was unhappy with regards to how much time the project had taken to complete, which by all accounts was a new project and really didn't take long to complete. The COO went on to say that he did not want to terminate me and would allow me to resign if I wanted to. It was December, and Christmas was but a couple of weeks away, and I remember thinking as I was walking to my office to gather my personal belongings; how would my family survive this new information. While taking that long and often silent walk back to my office the COO explained that none of this was his fault and that he was just following orders, he shook my hand and with his head hanging down, he quickly walked away.

Shortly after gathering my personal things, I walked to my car which seemed like an eternity in anticipation of the equally long drive home. I got into my car and immediately started to cry because I was literally more disappointed and humiliated rather than upset because I had given years of my life to this organization and had worked very diligently to maintain my department as a premiere department in that organization. I called my wife and explained to her what had just happened and she comforted me and reminded me that the CEO was known to be a bully as I had described the CEO's behavior to my family over the years at the dinner table often referring to the CEO as a dictator of sorts. My wife continued to explain that she was not surprised and knew that I would definitely recover from this situation. I must say, at that moment, I wish that I had the same confidence in myself that my wife had for me.

To put things into perspective, I must first describe the personality of the CEO of this particular organization. With all due respect, she's a brilliant thinker with incredible insight; however, the major flaw in all of this is that she preferred to lead by fear rather than by inclusion. To illustrate this, it was a known fact that this CEO engaged in yelling tirades in the office so that everyone in the vicinity heard her and thus permeated the fear. Also, she was known for giving projects to staff members to complete and when they were finished and praised by others for having done an incredible job on the project, the CEO was often jealous if the praises were not given to her even though she hadn't helped on any of the projects in any way shape or form.

Years later, I learned from a former colleague that the Talent Search Committee was thriving and that the only thing that had changed was the name, it was now called the Talent Search Team, but all of the requirements, methods and details that my group had developed continued to be utilized by the organization. Remember that I said that this CEO loved to be praised; well I also learned that while being praised for developing the recruitment plan, I forgot to give praises to the CEO and to mention to the masses that it was her idea. I was also informed that because I had not praised her; that was the real reason that I was asked to resign.

For months after being asked to leave an organization that I gave my heart and soul to everyday with regards to my work ethic, I continued to overanalyze the situation often replaying over and over what I could have done better in the situation. I began to stress over the fact that I had done something wrong even though that CEO was responsible for my demise given the fact that she was a known bipolar candidate. The only thing that got me through this ordeal was to remember what I'd heard from my high school English Teacher many years ago, which is the same quote at the beginning of this chapter, "We are all faced with a series of great opportunities brilliantly disguised as insoluble problems." The moral of this story is that opportunities are sometimes brilliantly disguised as setbacks. However, the trick is to make adjustments when those setbacks are presented to you.

With this message of hope, I actually began to feel better and my thoughts began to shift into something positive. It is easy to forget that when we're thinking, it's just a thought and not our reality. As crazy as it seems, as humans we forget that when we are thinking it is effortless because that is something that we are constantly doing like blinking our eyes. I'll bet that you were not even conscious of blinking your eyes until I said it, were you? Thinking works in a very similar way and I will discuss this more in chapter seven when I talk about the power of believing, but for now, consider your thoughts as something that steers your career.

Your thoughts are like magnets in that they attract to you what you constantly ponder. I know that it's hard to believe, and as I have stated before, I use to be the consummate skeptic; however, through research and belief, I've come to understand the remarkable thing that most of us sometimes or another have taken for granted – the mind. As complex as the mind seems, its powers are relatively understandable. The more you think about something good or bad, you will call those thoughts into actions and will ultimate experience them as your realities. To illustrate this, according to Earl Nightingale, author of *The Strangest Secret*, we become and experience what we think about the most. In a passage from his book, he explained the following:

> Now how does it work? Why do we become what we think about? Well, I'll tell you how it works, as far as we know. Now to do this I want To tell you about a situation that parallels the human mind. Suppose a Farmer has some land and it's good, fertile land.

> Now the land gives the Farmer a choice. He may plant in that land whatever he chooses; the land doesn't care. It's up to the farmer to make the decision. Now remember we're comparing the human mind with the land. Because the mind, like the land, doesn't

care what you plant in it. It will return what you plant, but it doesn't care what you plant.

Now let's say that the farmer has two seeds in his hand. One is a seed of corn, the other is nightshade – a deadly poison. He digs two little holes in the earth and plants both seeds: one corn, the other nightshade. He covers up the holes, waters and takes care of the land, and what will happen?

Invariably, the land will return what is planted. As written in the Bible: "As you sow, so shall you reap". Remember, the land doesn't care. It will return poison in just as wonderful as it will corn. So up come the two plants one corn, one poison.

Now the human mind is far more fertile, far more incredible and mysterious than the land, but it works the same way. It doesn't care what we plant – success, failure; a concrete worthwhile goal, or confusion, misunderstanding, fear, anxiety and so on. But what we plant, it will return to us.

~Earl Nightingale

After leaving that organization, and experiencing humiliation at the hands of that crazy CEO, I had a lot of time on my hands so I decided to read as much as I could on motivational topics, movies, songs, physics and the powers of the mind. I decided to think positive thoughts about the type of job that I wanted and in approximately four months after thinking positive thoughts about the dream job that I wanted, something unimaginable happened.

I will never forget, I was out having dinner with some friends and received a phone call on my cell phone. The voice on the other line explained that he had received my resume and wanted to know if I was interested in interviewing for a contractor position at NASA's Johnson Space Center. At first, I thought that it was some type of joke that my friends were playing on me because of my newfound reality of being positive; therefore, I immediately hung up the phone. However, the person called me back and before I could say stop playing games, the person on the phone said that he was a recruiter and apologized for having called me so late in the evening. He gave me a call back number and scheduled a meeting with me a few days later. This was all puzzling to me considering that I had never contemplated working at Johnson Space Center or even in the Aerospace Industry, because this would truly be a dream job for us dreamers. To make a long story short, I started working at Johnson Space Center a few weeks later. From that day, I became dedicated to thinking positive outcomes regardless of the situation.

Some years later, while vacationing, my wife and I decided to take in a movie; however, the movie that we wanted to see had already started before we could get our tickets, so we decided to see another movie which was unfamiliar to us named *Larry Crowne* co-written by Tom Hanks and Nia Vardalos. This turned out to be a very good movie in that it portrayed Larry Crowne, a middle aged military veteran who was fired from his job at a big name department store despite his seniority and satisfactory work, because the company has decided that his lack of college education impedes any chance of advancement. Larry, who is divorced and lives alone, cannot find a job and could lose his house. However, Larry does the unthinkable by returning to college and the rest is history, this was an excellent movie about bouncing back from adversity, this is a must see movie.

Imagine being middle aged and working for a company for which you have giving your heart and soul to, only to learn that today is your last day. What would you do? How would you recover? Many of us would want to give up and would probably make every excuse known to man as to why they should give up, instead of bouncing back. Just like Larry Crowne, I was in a similar situation as described in this chapter, and trust me, bouncing back from adversity is a huge part of survival in the workplace. Also, I've learned that while going through setbacks, it's very wise not only to engage yourself in positive thinking, but to immerse yourself into positive things such as movies like Larry Crowne, motivational books and the likes so as to keep your mind focused on becoming better. When that COO told me that my services were no longer needed, albeit devastating, I had to refocus my priorities and make certain adjustments in my life.

In addition to adjustments, you must recover quickly and in order for you to do this; you will need three things to help you maneuver through the difficulty which lies ahead. You will need a mantra, some understanding and love for your enemies and a plan. A mantra is something that will motivate you to change such as a chant, a song, etc. mine is a theme song, *The Payback* by James Brown. This song describes a person who plans to take revenge against someone who has betrayed them. Now, I'm not the kind of person to seek revenge against anyone nor do I condone such behavior; however, when I hear the beat and open instrumental arrangement of this particular song I get really fired up and motivated to succeed especially after someone has tried to purposefully block me from getting something desirable or has deliberately treated me unfairly. The trick when utilizing a song like this, you must not think about harming another person because that will put you in the category with them. Instead, you must focus on getting the type of dream job that you desire or whatever else it is that you're seeking.

Next, you will need a lot of understanding and love for your enemies, antagonists, haters and the likes. I know that this may seem strange to love someone that is causing harm to you in the workplace or in general for that matter. However, consider all of the transgressions taken against people such as Dr. Martin Luther King, Jr. or Mohandas

Gandhi and how they had to endure, make adjustments and overcome life threatening attacks on them as well as their families. In 1957, at Dexter Avenue Baptist Church, in Montgomery Alabama, Dr. King delivered an incredible speech, *Loving Your Enemies*, during a time of racial discrimination and inequality in America. Dr. King's speech described how and why we should love our enemies, in an excerpt from that speech, Dr. King explained:

> And this is what Jesus means, I think, in this very passage when he says, "Love your enemy." And it's significant that he does not say, "Like your enemy." Like is a sentimental something, an affectionate something. There are a lot of people that I find it difficult to like. I don't like what they do to me. I don't like what they say about me and other people. I don't like their attitudes. I don't like some of the things they're doing. I don't like them. But Jesus says love them. And love is greater than like. Love is understanding, redemptive goodwill for all men, so that you love everybody, because God loves them. You refuse to do anything that will defeat an individual, because you have *agape* in your soul. And here you come to the point that you love the individual who does the evil deed, while hating the deed that the person does. This is what Jesus means when he says, "Love your enemy." This is the way to do it. When the opportunity presents itself when you can defeat your enemy, you must not do it.
>
> Now for the few moments left, let us move from the practical how to the theoretical why. It's not only necessary to know how to go about loving your enemies, but also to go down into the question of

why we should love our enemies. I think the first reason that we should love our enemies, and I think this was at the very center of Jesus' thinking, is this: that hate for hate only intensifies the existence of hate and evil in the universe. If I hit you and you hit me and I hit you back and you hit me back and go on, you see, that goes on ad infinitum. It just never ends. Somewhere somebody must have a little sense, and that's the strong person. The strong person is the person who can cut off the chain of hate, the chain of evil. And that is the tragedy of hate that it doesn't cut it off. It only intensifies the existence of hate and evil in the universe. Somebody must have religion enough and morality enough to cut it off and inject within the very structure of the universe that strong and powerful element of love.

~Dr. Martin Luther King, Jr.

It works, you can't move on from a setback if you are filled with hate, resentment or other negative things, as it will cloud your judgment in most cases, and will not open you up to receive other opportunities that are waiting for you. Just think if I would have focused on trying to seek some type of revenge against that CEO for terminating me, I would have missed out on a better opportunity that was waiting for me the entire time. Just as Dr. King stated; if the opportunity presented itself for me to defeat or harm someone, just like that CEO, I wouldn't have, for the sheer fact that I would have missed out on a grand opportunity to get ahead in a different organization.

Finally, you will need a plan if you are to get from where you are to where you want to be. Remember, prayer is a great tool, but you also need a plan of action to get that dream job or position. To be perfectly honest, because we are human, there are going to be times that you feel like giving up and throwing in the towel sort to speak. I would encourage you from experience not to do so. There were many occasions when I was terminated that I felt like giving up and my emotions seemingly drained all of my hope. However, not only did I know that there was a plan for me, but I worked diligently at bringing that dream job into existence. I updated my resume, spoke to numerous contacts that I made over the years, remained positive and most of all; I continued to go on with my life as though nothing had happened. I got up in the morning put on my suit as though I were going to work and although I wasn't physically going to the office; I kept getting up in the morning as if I were. Also, I continued to research companies and most importantly, took care of my health which segues into the next segment.

## MINDING YOUR TEMPLE

Consider this; if your body was a major corporation, then your brain would be the CEO of that corporation. As discussed earlier, CEO's are responsible for directing the business also to provide overall leadership to the organization by establishing direction, overseeing senior executives, and to function as the organization's primary contact for outside entities. CEO's are at the helm of organizations and influences a great deal of people. If they make bad decisions, sometimes the entire organization may suffer. Just as with your mind, if your thoughts are cloudy or negative, this could mean that your entire body may suffer.

To illustrate this point, think of working for an organization and suddenly you had to make an adjustment which might include being subject to a reduction in force or layoff as it is often referred to or worst, let's say you were terminated. After receiving the message that you were terminated, you find the nearest bar and begin to drink to the point of inebriation. Later, you leave that bar completely intoxicated get into your car and proceed to drive home. On the drive home you crash into a light post only to find yourself in the hospital awakened a week later, paralyzed from the neck down. This is a very sad but real example in that there have been numerous individuals that have taken this course of action in dealing with setbacks. Surely, the end is not what was intended based on the circumstances involved. This is not a smart adjustment based on a setback, is it? Just as the CEO of an organization makes decisions, so do you with regards to everything; remember, you have choices, and your business (your body) is depending on you to make good choices.

The mind is a complex tool that requires a lot of nourishment as well as nurturing. Also, you must guard it with all of your strength against negative influences including negative thoughts and substances. *Substance abuse* also known as drug abuse is a patterned use of (drug) in which the user consumes the substance in amounts or with methods neither approved nor supervised by medical professionals. Substance abuse/drug abuse is not limited to mood altering or psycho-active drugs. If an activity is performed using the objects against the rules and policies of the matter (as in steroids for performance enhancement in sports), it is also called substance abuse. Therefore mood-altering and psychoactive substances are not the only type of drug abuse. Substance abuse often includes problems with impulse control and impulse behavior. In addition, taking care of your temple not only means reframing from substance but it also requires education, meditation and relaxation to help with impulse control.

Learn as much as you can where you are in your current situation, it is preparing you for your next move. Know that knowledge is powerful, when you know something; it is sometimes painful almost like a slow death if not acted upon. When I was growing up; my mother always said no pain no gain, often referring to studying and doing well in school. My mother made it mandatory that books were an essential part of our daily regimen, when I think about how diligent my mother was with regards to education, it makes me very happy because she saw something in us during my elementary years that my siblings and I could not have imagined at such an early age. My mother was not a fortune teller; however, she knew that education would permeate every aspect of our lives for years to come.

Besides believing and relationship building, education is the epitome of what it takes to get the job that you desire. When I say education, I'm not just referring to formal text book knowledge, with education also comes *"street sense"* as my grandmother use to refer to common sense which means that learning is also about observation. Some of the greatest research in the world has stemmed from someone observing something which translated into an action. If you don't believe me, just look around you at all of the airplanes, buildings, technologies and other inventions, all of this was because someone exercised their learning and wanting to do something great.

Next, meditation is the process of training the mind and/or inducing a mode of consciousness. The term meditation refers to a broad variety of practices (much like the term sports) which range from techniques designed to promote relaxation, building internal energy, getting closer to God and so forth, to more technical exercises targeted at developing compassion, love, patience, generosity, forgiveness and more far-reaching goals such as effortless sustained single-pointed concentration, single-pointed analysis, and an indestructible sense of well-being while engaging in any and all of life's activities. Meditation brings us into a different realm of thinking so as to call into existence the things that we desire including a better life, a better job, becoming a better person, and so forth. As I have stated earlier, learning and observation are essential qualities to have in order to steer your desires into action; however, constant meditation brings those desires into fruition. A strong believer in Christian meditation, Saint Padre Pio stated: *"Through the study of books one seeks God; by meditation one finds him*". Thus, it is very important for you to set aside some time daily to meditate on the things that you want.

Finally, relaxation quiets the mind, just as a body builder needs relaxation to recover muscle tissue; we too need a period of relaxation so that our mind, body and spirit can recover. It is very crucial to get rest and know that God continues to do the work for us. God desires rest for us because it does not come naturally to us. To rest, we have to trust that God will take care of things for us. We have to trust that, if we take a day off, the world will not stop turning on its axis. From the beginning (Genesis 3), when we decided that we would start making all the decisions, mankind has become more tense and less able to relax. It was disobedience in the Garden of Eden that started this problem. But obedience now will bring the rest that God so desires for us (Hebrews 4:11). If one of the definitions of *"relax"* is *"to make less tense, rigid or firm,"* then relaxing our grip on our own lives, jobs, careers, families, etc, and giving them over to God in faith and belief is the best way to relax.

## Minding Your Business

Minding your business takes on several meanings, when I was growing up and adults were engaged in a conversation, it could be very detrimental for children to interrupt. However, if they were brave enough to interrupt, they were quickly greeted by *"mind your business"*, meaning that the children should refrain from listening to the adult conversation and redirect their attention elsewhere. Another meaning that is befitting to this segment deals with taking care of your affairs as they pertain to your relationships at work, your understanding of business in general and your identity or brand.

I've discussed getting connected already and what that entails, but for the sake of business, you need to know whether you realize it or not, you are your own personal walking business. Just as any business, not only must you have positive relationships with people, but you must be a positive business altogether. The opposite of negative people, positive people have unique habits in that they are aware and know how to fit in, in other words, not only do they understand the culture of the organization, but they know how to navigate to engage themselves, always thinking one level up or ahead. They are often acquainted with the likes of people who are working in the position or have achieved the success or status that they want to have. This is a science of sorts, and once you have mastered this, you will open yourself up to new horizons and levels, believe me, it works. The trick in all of this is not to be snobbish as you become successful, remember, everything is about attraction, good things attract good things, so if you are acting like you are better than someone else, this evokes negativity and you will attract negativity.

Another thing that is crucial in building relationships that most people often misinterpret; is to know that everyone in whom you work with are not your friends, for the most part, they are either colleagues or co-workers, you have a very short list of friends in the workplace. To illustrate this point, my wife often refers to everyone at work as a friend or everyone that she went to high school with as a friend; needless to say, I always intervene and remind her that those individuals are co workers and former classmates. Let's face it, friends are tried and true, meaning that there are certain distinctions that makes someone a friend. For example, when you are experiencing tough times, perhaps financial situations, a friend might assist you with support. Or, how many times have you seen in the media where someone is being ridiculed, well a friend will come to your aid even at the cost of being humiliated themselves.

Having said that, it is equally important for you to stop telling your co workers, colleagues, boss and others at work about your every move, to include personal endeavors, dreams, personal goals, financial situation and desires. I'm not suggesting for you to suddenly become a mute, if you do, people would surely think that something was wrong with you. However, what I am suggesting is that you refrain from discussing your personal mission, vision and values with others all the time.

To illustrate this point, my sister-in-law, a school teacher in Houston was becoming very frustrated at the school that she was working at for years. Therefore, during the summer, typically the time off that teachers have, she started looking for another position at a different school and put in several applications. As a result, she was called in for an interview at a new school and was so excited about the prospects of working at the new school; she decided to tell several of her teacher friends (really co workers) to inform them about the new opportunity. Several weeks had gone by, and she was getting a bit nervous because she hadn't heard from her prospective employer and the new school year was about to start. Therefore, she decided to give the principal of the new school a call to inquire about the status of her application. The principal informed my sister-in-law that the position had been filled. Guess who got the new job? Correct, one of her friends (I mean co-workers) that she talked with about the new opportunity, because the friends (co-workers) were equally unhappy at the old school as well.

In minding your business, there is a cost associated with doing business. Growing up, I often heard the phrase *"It's just business and nothing personal"*, and for me, that's the mentality that I have embodied when it comes to the workplace in an effort to survive. One thing that I've learned over the years is that you must never under any circumstances give all of your heart and soul to any organization that is in a position to terminate, demote, trade or otherwise affect you. The reason being is that the saddest thing in life is to work for an organization most of your life only to find out one day that your services are no longer needed. Even if you are a stellar employee, athlete, etc. you are expendable.

Consider this, Peyton Manning by all intents and purposes; is one of the greatest quarterbacks to ever play in the National Football League; however, at the end of the 2011 football season, his services were no longer needed in Indianapolis. Okay, I'm sure that the owner didn't tell Peyton Manning those exact words; however, you get the point. Even if you're great, there are times when organizations tend to forget all of the good things that you've done for them over the years. Remember, you don't have to be a professional athlete to be traded for someone else. People are always being vetted for your job, believe it or not. Now, that's not to cause a panic; however, you should be aware of these facts so that your feelings are not hurt if it happens to you. After all, *"It's just business and nothing personal"*.

The last in this segment of minding your business, is to have a unique brand or identity. Consider this; most product brands are so popular that people often use one name to describe similar products. To illustrate this point, how many times have you heard someone sneeze and then ask for a Kleenex, well a Kleenex is a particular brand of tissue. Or how many times have you seen a child scrape his or her knee and then ask for a Band-Aid, well a Band-Aid is a particular brand of bandage. The point that I'm trying to make is that you are a product and believe it or not, you are either in demand or not. Therefore, it is critical for you to work on your weaknesses as well as redefine your strengths. Just as companies reinvent themselves from time to time, you must do the same in order to survive the rat race at work.

There is a ton of research out there about ways to reinvent yourself, keep in mind that reinventing yourself may not necessarily mean that you go out and buy a new wardrobe or a CD to help you look or speak better. However, it may entail that you hit your restart button in order to change the game at work. This means a difference in how you do your job and how you connect with and relate to people. This requires much work and dedication considering that you may have been in the same game sort to speak, for many years.

If you're like me, you may not be involved with all of the social media out there, considering the time that it takes to keep up with this person or that person, or it may seem altogether like a complete waste of time to you. However, if you use social media in a different manner such that it is a tool by which you change lives or influence those in charge, then you are truly on to something, a power move. For example, what started out as a small communication model, blogging has now captivated many viewers and has become a lucrative tool for professionals. Therefore, you must keep up with what's current in order to carve out your place in the game. Remember work is a game and there are winners, losers and people just playing to play; why not be in it to win it.

## Give and You Shall Receive

When making adjustments in life, some of us forget that the most important ingredient when waiting for something such as a better opportunity requires a giving heart and gratitude. You may not believe this, but the more that you give, the more shall you receive. If it's a job, career or position that you want, having gratitude will help the process move along faster. There's something magical about gratitude that opens doors to the flood gates of whatever it is that you desire. When I say give, I'm not just referring to monetary value; I'm also talking about your time, energy and efforts. Give; and it will be given to you. A good measure, pressed down, shaken together and running over, will be poured into your lap. For with the measure you use, it will be measured to you (Luke 6:38).

When I loss my job, I was devastated and felt like giving up on everything; however, I decided in order to keep busy, I would volunteer in the community and engage myself in giving of my time freely. I tutored students, volunteered at non-profit agencies you name it, I was there. With all of this busy work, I forgot that I was unemployed and then all of a sudden, the flood gate of job offers opened up to me and the rest was history.

*"Always do right, this will gratify some and astonish the rest."*
~ MARK TWAIN

# CHAPTER 6

# ALWAYS, ALWAYS, ALWAYS, DO THE RIGHT THING

A S A CHILD, I WITNESSED my mother demonstrating doing the right thing and it changed my life for the better. I was in elementary and one day after school, we stopped by the grocery store on the way home and while in the grocery store, a lady dropped her purse on the floor while shopping but was unaware that she had loss her purse. Inside the purse was an envelope full of money, I mean there was a lot of money, nearly one thousand dollars; also, there was a photo ID in the wallet. My mother is a very honest person and immediately canvassed what seemed to be the entire store in an attempt to locate the owner of the purse, without having any luck; my mother went to customer service, called the manager and explained to him what she had found in the store. Needless to say, the manager immediately made an announcement on the store's PA system and shortly thereafter, an elderly lady came to the manager's booth. As it turned out, the lady explained that she had just cashed her husband's monthly retirement check which was their only source of income and was shopping for groceries for the month. I'll never forget, my mother explaining to me and my siblings, the importance of doing the right thing.

Less than a week later, a similar incident happened to my mother. In a rush to pick us up from school, my mother stopped by that same store and after paying for her items, she had accidentally forgotten her purse at the check-out counter. My mother didn't realize what had happened until we returned home when she was attempting to get the house keys from her purse; which she suddenly realized wasn't there. In a mad dash back to the store, she went to the cash register only to be directed to the manager's booth. That same manager had retrieved her purse and when she walked up to the booth he had an enormous smile on his face as if to say what goes around comes around. My mother had shown good faith a week earlier and it was returned back to her. In addition, that store manager gave my mother a voucher for free items for being such a positive role model for his employees.

## It Comes Back To You

Ever since I witnessed my mother as a child in that grocery store, I've always tried to do what's right throughout the years. For one thing, you never know what someone else is going through. That elderly lady in the store depended on that money to buy groceries for the month. Also, it's not just about doing what's right in the community; you also have to do what's right in every walk of life. However, since the focus of this book is about work, you can take some of the positive attributes that you perform in the community and bring them into the workplace.

It's like a magnetic force, when you do right good things are drawn to you, and the opposite, when you do wrong, bad things are drawn to you. To illustrate this, either I'm a target for some sort of testing on right and wrong or, I'm just the luckiest person in the world. For years, I have been going to professional sporting events and whenever I have to go up to the ticket booth to purchase a ticket, I'm always informed by the ticket representative that I have somehow already paid for a ticket when I haven't. It would make perfect sense for me to realize if I had purchased a ticket or not considering that I'm the one spending the money. When presented with that, most people would have walked into the stadium fully knowing that they hadn't purchased a ticket. Not me, I'm the person who literally stands there and argues the case that I want to pay for my ticket, often holding up the line and being ridiculed by impatient fans. As luck would have it, I would always pay my money and then something incredible would happen, like the time I argued with a ticket rep and after walking into the stadium, I was asked if I wanted to go up to the press box, it seemed that the team's owner wanted to get in touch with the fans on that particular day.

On another occasion, when I was in college, I was standing in line at Dillard's Department Store waiting to pay a bill and I realized that I was mistakenly in the wrong line. It seemed that I was in the line to be interviewed by the Operations Manager for the upcoming holiday temporary jobs. Well, again, as luck would have it, when the Operations Manager came out of the office he asked who's next and everyone looked at me. I was embarrassed and explained that I was waiting in line to pay a bill. However, the Manager asked if I would like to interview for a job and the rest was history; I worked several holiday seasons as a temporary seasonal worker for that store.

When I first came into the workforce, I'm referring to my first job where I was able to go out on my own and take care of myself, I discovered that it was really easy and necessary to stand out from the crowd by doing just a little bit more than what I was supposed to do. More importantly, I enjoyed doing the right thing as oppose to doing what was easy. Now, I'll admit that I've had my fair share of doing wrong things and have paid for each of them in one way or another. However, I will profess that I have done far more good than I have bad, as I have experienced firsthand that you cannot do wrong without it coming back to you.

Years ago, my boss promised that because of my work ethic, I was next in line for a promotion. In anticipation of the promotion, my boss moved me from the world of cubicles into my own office even though I had not officially received the promotion yet. Needless to say, I was very excited and finally realized that all of my hard work was finally paying off. To show my appreciation to my boss for having such confidence in me, I started taking on more work to the point that I was even doing her job at times. As a result, members of upper-management started noticing me and were very impressed with my work and even asked my boss why I hadn't been promoted yet. Also, it was rumored that an executive wanted me to join their team.

Well, the rumors became a reality, and it was a requirement that in order for me to move to another area within the organization, my boss would have to give me a letter of recommendation. Not only would I be getting a promotion, but I would be on the same level of management as my boss. I was thrilled because after all, I knew that I had worked really hard especially taking on extra assignments for my boss, that was a great day. About a week later, I was called into the office of what I thought was going to be my new boss only to be informed that due to the recommendation, I would not being getting the assignment. This was very puzzling to me because I knew that my boss was going to give me a glowing recommendation. The downside to this is that employees at that organization are not allowed to see or even challenge recommendation letters. However, it's good to have friends in high places, because I learned that my boss due to me having an opportunity to be on the same level had trashed me in the recommendation letter.

I went back to work in my old position and I didn't even get the original promotion that I was promised due to the fact that it would look bad for my boss to promote me after trashing me to upper management. I went back to work, never informing my boss that I was aware of what she had done to me. It was like dying a very slow death considering that I had to go to work each day knowing what type of person that I was working for. Never do bad things to people, because it will always come back to you, shortly after leaving that organization, I learned that my boss was terminated for misconduct.

Lesson learned, know your enemies, they may even be in your office working next to you. According to David D'Alessandro, author of *Career Warfare*, "You will make some enemies without lifting a finger, simply by virtue of who you are. You will make enemies because you are short or tall, or because you are a woman or you are a person of color. You will make enemies because of your education – either you didn't go to the type of school that's in favor now, or you went to a better school than your peers and will suffer because they are jealous. You will make enemies because you work for a certain department or for a certain individual who is the sworn enemy of someone else. You will make enemies just because you exist."

In short, it's also good to have spies in high places; I would have never suspected that my boss could have done something like that to me. I'm not suggesting that you become *007* or someone like that; however, it's a good practice to have someone in the know that you can depend on for authentic information. According to Sun Tzu, *The Art of War*, "Knowledge of the enemy's disposition can only be obtained from other men." Your biggest weapon in the workplace is awareness, in order to survive enemies; you will need to be aware that they exist in the first place.

## WORKPLACE RESPONSIBILITIES

Executives, managers and those in supervisory roles alike have far more responsibilities than that of daily operations and being in charge of people. Management also has the social responsibility of treating employees fairly, respectful, with dignity and most of all, having some air of integrity. This responsibility also relates to satisfactory work in that management is responsible for building and maintaining harmonious relationships between themselves and their subordinates. This responsibility also includes refraining from abusing their authority on subordinates.

When I finally became a member of management, I decided to go against the grain which meant that I'd be less demanding, less dictatorial, less crazy and more involved with my employees and their well-being. Let's face it, when treated fairly, employees will go to the ends of the earth to protect you from harm and to make you look good. However, there are those employees who love to abuse and take advantage of the system which segues into those responsibilities of employees (staff members) to their employer.

Just as employers have a social responsibility to employees, employees have a responsibility to their employer which extends beyond hours of work. Employees have a moral obligation to their employer as well as their co-workers. Consider this, if an employee takes advantage of the system or manipulates the rules and regulations to fit their own personal needs that are not emergencies; for example, misusing the attendance policy by not coming to work or having a habit of missing days such as every other Friday, this is bad for business because not only is the employee missing work, but their absence often affects co-workers in that someone has to absorb the work of that missing employee. Also, some employees are also known to take advantage of Federally protected statutes such as FMLA and other mandates. This too is not good because it can affect an organization's bottom line which could affect a great deal of people to include possible reductions in staff members, lay-offs and other budgetary constraints.

Therefore, if you are engaging in this type of behavior from a management perspective or from an employee perspective, you really should consider what's at stake for others at the organization. It's a pretty selfish act and a high cost to pay for doing the wrong things. You should never play the system even when you can, because it will ultimately come back to haunt you and could possibly affect others.

*"If you can! All things are possible for ones who believe."*

~ MARK 9:23

# CHAPTER 7

# BELIEVE

ONE OF MY FAVORITE PASSAGES from the bible is Mark 9:23 *"And Jesus said to him, if you can! All things are possible for ones who believe"*. For many years, I did not understand the power of believing; in fact, I thought that everything good that happened to me was somehow because of something that I did or better yet, that I deserved. As a child, I often frequented church and read the bible, but it wasn't until I started doing research that the magic of believing incorporated with the teachings of the bible, started to make sense to me. This was an awesome revelation and has come to mean a great deal to me in my spiritual life, personal life as well as my professional life. Inside my home, outside in the flower beds and throughout my office at work, you will find artwork, frames, book marks, you name it, all with the word **B-E-L-I-E-V-E** on them in some form or fashion. Not only do I have artwork with the word believe inscribed, but one of my favorite songs is *"I Believe"* by recording artists, The Sounds of Blackness, which is a very motivational song. My favorite artwork in my home dawns the hall on canvass and reads:

> *The future*
> *belongs to those who*
> *believe in the beauty*
> *of their dreams*

## BELIEVE

The word believe is visible, and is a constant reminder to me, my family and to anyone that enters our home that whatever they are going through, the power of belief will make it happen for them or remove it from their lives. Although believing in something is powerful; however, in wanting something, you cannot waiver back and forth or be unsure in your thoughts, you must have absolute certainty that you will get whatever it is that you are wanting. Believing in something also means, "To have confidence in the truth, the existence, or the reliability of something, although without absolute proof that one is right in doing so: Only if one believes in something can one act purposefully."

In many organizations, you will find leaders as well as workers that are truly unsuccessful and most of all, who do not remain with their organizations to tell their stories. This is largely because employees alike sometimes think that they are the driving force behind their success and at that point, they start to spiral down due to arrogance and a lack of gratitude. Turn on the television and look at the news and see how many executives are being fired or have gone through some sort of senate or congressional hearing for wrongdoings. This is a problem and is very prevalent throughout many organizations worldwide. The same happens to employees when they feel that it is okay to manipulate the system in an effort to get ahead. Don't be like these individuals; trust me, success without belief is short lived.

The reverse to this is that there are very few executives as well as employees that are successful. This is because they understand certain laws within the universe that are not manmade. Look at some of the most successful people in the world such as Warren Buffet, Bill Gates, Carlos Helu, Larry Ellison, Christy Walton, Mukesh Ambani, Oprah Winfrey, Mark Zuckerberg, Shawn "Jay-Z" Carter, Indra Nooyi and Steve Jobs just to name a few; regardless of their professions or backgrounds, these individuals have been mentioned in *Forbes Magazine* among either the richest or most powerful people in the world. Also, they are all on a very short list, but all have the same recipe for success in some way or another. For the most part, that recipe is the constant drive and belief at succeeding in their respective disciplines, which for all of these particular individuals came to fruition.

It is not by luck that these individuals became successful or by some entity giving them a chance to succeed, their success can be summed up in one word – belief. It may be difficult for some people to accept that these individuals just believed in something and it manifested. Well, it's real, just as the sun sets and rises, so does a thought, and when put into action; any, and everything is possible if you believe. If you do not put your thoughts into action, they will set like the sun, but will only rise once put into motion again.

The difference between your thoughts and the sun is that the sun rises automatically, whereas we have to work at it. Now, this is not to say that once you stop putting effort into something that it is gone forever, once you bring that back into action, the process will start all over again. Consider this, there's been several people who've become incredible rich and successful and loss everything because they were not taking care of business. However, once they started putting their beliefs back into motion they rebounded and got everything back again.

## The Science Behind Believing

There is a science to believing, when I was in high school, I wasn't really good at physics, not because I couldn't do the work, but because I didn't understand certain laws and concepts surrounding physics. However, after studying books and information on the power of believing and similar readings, a light came on and it was as though I understood the concepts of physics my entire life. Physics play a huge role in our daily lives, consider this, if asked, most people do not stop to think about physics or the laws governed by the science. For the most part, as humans, we take for granted the essence of our existence. For example, how often can you honestly say that you appreciate physics and the constant laws at work? Put another way, we may not appreciate certain laws, but most of us will definitely abide by them.

You do not have to believe me when I say that certain physical laws are unequivocally accepted as true. For example, you do not have to believe in Sir Isaac Newton's concepts on gravity, energy and force to know that if you were to jump from a 20 story building, you would surely hit the ground. Even if you're not a scientist, mathematician, etc. you believe this theory as the gospel. Even if you do not believe this, I don't think that anyone would try to disprove the law of gravity by jumping off a building in an effort to challenge this fact. Would you?

The same holds for our minds and bodies, in that we are all energy and force, a moving current which attracts things to us. You cannot see gravity, but you believe it's there, just as you cannot see currents, energy, etc. but you know it's there based on some outcome. For example, while working at NASA, I often had the pleasure of meeting and talking with several scientists, engineers and astronauts about the laws of science and was always amazed at how knowledgeable they were regarding this topic. Also, it was an incredible feat for the Space Shuttle to launch into space and all of those involved with its efforts, never questioning how a shuttle could lift off from earth and go into space and return to earth. It was as though all of this was second nature to everyone involved. Not really! This was a thought (belief) put into motion which came to fruition.

These currents are also prevalent in the workplace and can be dangerous if manifested by ill-intentions. For example, how many times have you heard a co-worker talking negatively about the boss, management, another co-worker, etc. not a good feeling is it? If you listen to this gossip long enough, you will find yourself equally talking negatively about those same individuals that your co-worker has made reference to. The only problem with this is that typically, the person that is speaking negatively about another; usually suffers the setbacks themselves. And you know what? Often times those same individuals that you are talking negatively about are being promoted, getting better opportunities, their own offices, you name it. And in some cases, not because they deserve these things, but because those who talk negatively about these individuals are given them constant energy because they are the topics of discussion. Turn on the television, people such as actors, singers, performers who've done something wrong, continue to be in the media, in some cases receiving multimillion dollar offers because of all of the attention, press and energy given to them by the viewers and the media.

According to Prentice Mulford, in *Thoughts are Things*, writes, "When people come together and in any way talk out their ill-will towards others they are drawing to themselves with ten-fold power an injurious thought current. Because the more minds united on any purpose the more power do they attract to affect that purpose. The thought current so attracted by those chronic complainers, grumblers and scandal mongers, will injure their bodies. Because whatever thought is most held in mind is most materialized in the body. If we are always thinking and talking of people's imperfections we are drawing to us ever of that thought current, and thereby incorporating into ourselves those very imperfections". In the reverse, the same holds for good thoughts, the more we think and speak good things about others, the more positive things will manifest into our lives.

Another thing to consider is that as humans we are perfect, from the beginning, we were made perfect by God and disobedience caused us to engage in inappropriate behaviors. My wife and I recently went to the museum to view *"The Bodies Revealed Exhibition"* which showcases real human bodies , dissected and preserved to illustrate each body system and function. It was an amazing exhibit, in that we got a chance to see the human body from a different perspective. It was surreal to see the perfection of human bodies up close and personal. We both discussed how great God is to have made humans perfect and how we take this gift for granted. We constantly abuse our minds by thinking negative thoughts which in some cases brings ailments to the body. Knowing this, why then would you speak or think negative thoughts?

## OPPORTUNITY VS. BELIEVING

I know that most of you are probably thinking if it's that easy, why everyone isn't practicing the concept of believing in something to get it. To put this into perspective please consider that there is relatively a very small percentage of the world's population that are rich, successful, happy, etc and even in that percentage, a lot of people are not studying these principles but rather are practicing them unknowingly. Another thought might be; why are there people that are rich and successful never discussing the power of believing. Consider this, the sun rises every morning and regardless if a person is poor, rich, short, tall, happy, sad, etc. the sun shines on everyone without their efforts. For example, people who focus on a goal and is willing to do anything, within reason and the law, typically acquires what they are thinking about. The sun shines on all of us good or bad; we all start out with an opportunity to gain something. However, it is with belief that we receive that which we think about the most.

Some may argue that opportunity exists in the world and it is somehow blind luck or serendipity that causes people to get things. The universe doesn't negate thought; for example, have you ever heard someone say that they're going to pray for you after telling them that you're interviewing for a job, having problems at work, you're about to undergo a medical procedure and so forth and so on, that power comes from thought, a request to God for you to acquire something, to be healed from something or to be removed from something. Therefore, you do not have to necessarily apply efforts, perhaps someone else is praying for you to get a position, a raise, to be removed from a negative environment, a new home or recover from an ailment, etc. And when it is manifested, whether you believe it or not, I would encourage you to show some gratitude, because as quick as you receive something, it can be taken away in the blink of an eye. Remember, others may focus on believing that you will get something or be healed and those currents flow just as strong as if you were thinking about the situation yourself.

Opportunity and belief works hand and hand, meaning that you get opportunities because of what you believe. Thus, the power of believing brings those opportunities to you. Trust me, to most, I know that these concepts are difficult to understand and grasp, because at one point in my life I was very skeptical about most things of this nature; however, by studying and doing research I came to not only believe, but to understand how certain laws work. There are a very small percentage of people on this earth who are aware of these concepts. The same holds for belief, I'm sure that the majority of folks that are rich had to have thought and contemplated being successful, having it all, and that is why they are successful, they thought it into action, but have often based their successes on going to the right school, making the right contacts, etc, this is why people lose their success as fast as they obtain it.

Remember earlier in Chapter 2 when I discussed being at a conference and the speaker was talking about NASA; well, I attended that conference many years prior to working at NASA. I was so impressed by the information that I learned from that conference, and subconsciously I thought about NASA but not in the context of getting the job at that particular time. However, years later when I got the position, I didn't realize that I was calling the job at NASA into existence subconsciously. According to Joseph Murphy, *The Power of Your Subconscious Mind*, "William James, the father of American Psychology, said that the power to move the world is in your subconscious mind. Your subconscious is one with infinite intelligence and boundless wisdom. It is fed by hidden springs, and is called the law of life. Whatever you impress upon your subconscious mind, the latter will move heaven and earth to bring it to pass. You must, therefore, impress it with right ideas and constructive thought."

Now that's not to say to make a request in prayer and not work at getting what you want, because thoughts, the subconscious mind and prayer all work hand and hand. It requires some effort on your part; consider this, if your desire is to have a beautiful garden and you decide to plant flower seeds in the ground without watering the soil, you may never get that beautiful garden. Or, if you decide to water the ground once a month you may get something mediocre; remember, you reap what you sow and that is the gospel. Also in prayer, "Keep on asking, and you will receive what you ask for. Keep on seeking, and you will find. Keep on knocking, and the door will be opened to you."

*"Bury the dead, they stink up the joint"*
~ (Coughlin's Law, Cocktail 1988)

# Chapter 8

# Bury the Dead

I N HIGH SCHOOL, I WAS in drama and we performed *"Bury the Dead"* a play by Irwin Shaw, about a group of soldiers killed in a battle who refuse to be buried. This was my first experience in acting and this was a wonderful play in that the characters mostly soldiers talked about their experiences as though they were alive, although they are dead. This too happens to a lot of people who refuse to bury certain experiences such as setbacks, being terminated, bad bosses, even negative family members, you name it. The problem with all of this is that by living these experiences over and over, they are blocking those things such as that new job, better experiences, more money etc. from coming into their lives.

It's funny that I can remember and can recall certain things that I did in my youth and how those same things relate to the current situations that I've experienced as an adult. For example, when I was a kid, country singer Kenny Rogers made a song called *The Gambler*, and that song would always come on the radio and I loved the following lyrics:

> *"You got to know when to hold'em, know when to fold'em,*
> *Know when to walk away, know when to run.*
> *You never count your money when you're sittin' at the table.*
> *There'll be time enough for countin' when the dealin's done."*

These lyrics are priceless in that you can relate them to a game of poker, or you could use your imagination to relate the lyrics to life lessons, especially those pertaining to work. Consider this, when it comes to work, we are all gamblers in that we really are not sure if we are going to win or lose when it comes to sustainability, changes, etc. So, in essence you have to know when to hold'em (to keep your current position), know when to foldem' (look for another opportunity elsewhere), know when to walk away (plan to leave the organization) and know when to run (leave the organization immediately). There are many other songs that I often think about such as the Blues, which is a specific genre of music which often entails a lot of storytelling usually in someone's plight against something which usually ends up being sad, happy or funny, but most importantly, about how to move on.

The name of this book is Asleep at Work, which describes things that are often happening at work and provides insight into dealing with as well as addressing those concerns. However, now that you are aware of these things, I would encourage you to wake up, bury the dead that's holding you back and move on. There's nothing wrong with reminiscing about certain situations from the past that have affected you; in fact, that is a good reference point in letting you know that problems are real and that you can get through them and one day over them.

I've used a lot of different medians in this book such as movies and songs to describe certain situations as they relate to the workplace and how people in general have survived those situations. Earlier, I mentioned the movie *The Matrix*, and how its theme is about choices. Another aspect of the movie deals with certain revelations that are difficult for someone to fathom considering that most people go about their daily lives accepting their current situations as their realities. I will say that this newfound reality about the workplace may seem difficult at first when accepting certain situations such as dealing with political realities or understanding institutional denial, considering that you may have believed your current situation to be true for a very long time. However, I want to encourage everyone reading this book to believe in the power of success and to know that there is a higher power working on your side.

Another experience that you may encounter regarding your new found reality is a host of emotions from having dealt with certain situations at work for so long. The good thing is that you are not alone, several people including myself, have dealt with realities in the workplace and have been equally upset because at first; I too wasn't equipped with insight to deal with certain aspects of my career such as institutional denial, office politics and other nonsense that surrounds the sometimes forty plus hours work week. To best describe this, consider being awakened from a nightmare, it's not a good feeling at first, but then you feel relief because once you have awakened, you know that it was all a dream. According to the *American Psychiatric Association*, "A nightmare is an unpleasant dream that can cause a strong negative emotional response from the mind, typically fear or horror, but also despair, anxiety and great depression. The dream may contain situations of danger, discomfort, psychological or physical terror. Sufferers usually awaken in a state of distress and may be unable to return to sleep for a prolonged period of time."

The same is true when holding on to something in your past, if you do not let go of this experience, it may haunt you forever like a bad dream in that it will affect your ability to move on and you could be in this situation for a very long time and that's not good at all. Therefore, again, I highly encourage you to bury those things which are holding you back.

For some of you, if dealing with letting go of something is too painful to bear, I would suggest seeking counseling to deal with the situation. I know that some people might think that therapy is taboo, but it works if you find the right person. Also, in an effort to assist different personality types, the field of counseling is packaged under different names such as life coach, reinvention coach, career coach, etc. and if you can afford the likes, it's a good investment so long as you find the right person for the job. For others, there is a great deal of information out there in bookstores, on the web, at church and other groups that are less expensive and can give good results as well.

In closing, I want to encourage you to never give up on your dream job, as it is just around the corner and if you engage in the wrong things such as anxiety, substance abuse, complaining, vengeance just to name a few, you could be missing out on a life changing opportunity. Sure, there are people as I have mentioned; that I would love to have choked the wrongdoings out of them, but I know that they are getting their payment in full from a higher source. And as Frank Sinatra once quipped, *"The best revenge is massive success."* Live and work well my friends because that is what you were born to do; and you will never be satisfied unless you live and work well. Wake Up!

# AFTER THOUGHTS

Something is terribly wrong! Something is wrong with how we accept certain things especially conditions and arrangements at work. It is my hope that this book removes or at least alleviates some of the stress that employees are experiencing in the workplace. One thing that took me a long time to learn and was quite ironic is that life is very short and while we are here, we should appreciate every moment that we have. What's more, your time on any job is even shorter than your life expectancy. Therefore, everyday you should strive to enjoy and do the type of work that makes you happy. You will never be happy in any organization or job, no matter how much money you make, until you are happy and truly master the art of working well with others.

# THE CORPORATE FARM (SHORT STORY)

*Something we may **All** Experience in the Workplace*

The following short story represents a situation that most of us in the workplace have experienced or may experience at some point in their career. Like the chapters in this book, this short fable, *The Corporate Farm*, is a collection of wisdom that I have learned over the years from my observations in the workplace, from discussions with wise counsel, others whom I've consulted with through years of experience working in Human Resources and through my research as a Professor in the behavioral sciences.

The fictitious characters in this short story represent personalities that are often prevalent in the workplace and which are often presented more overtly when there's change or anticipated change:

**Doug Freelancer** – An arrogant, self promoting and backstabbing Pig who's willing to do anything to get ahead, to include sabotaging his colleagues.

**Craig Watcher** – A quiet but deadly Cow who's always proclaiming that, *"I'm just a cow on the farm, and my job is to eat the grass."*

**Dono Oblivion** – A Donkey who goes along with every situation in order to please everyone even at the expense of being humiliated himself.

**Ivanna Believe** – A Giraffe who represents difference and a positive outlook on work, people and the overall situation. Of note, I deliberately did not discuss this personality type in Chapter 4; *Political Realities*, because this type of person rarely exists in the workplace.

**Captain Seymour Upright** – An A&M educated Horse and (ex. Marine) who is sent to the Farm to conduct a climate assessment of the workers. He also represents authority and exhibits a great deal of wisdom at a critical moment.

T HE TIME IS 7:16 A.M. and the workers on the farm are becoming restless in the anticipation of Captain Upright who's scheduled to arrive on the Corporate Farm at 8:00 a.m. There's a great deal of angst amongst the employees because he's from the Executive Farm in Southfork, an exclusive Farm near Dallas, TX known for its demanding corporate executives. Due to ongoing budget cuts throughout the entire Farming Industry, Captain Upright has been sent to the Corporate Farm in West TX to lay off some of its workers. Interviews with workers will be one of the determining factors in who gets laid off. Captain Upright's first action on his agenda is to schedule one-on-one meetings with the employees to gauge the current climate and culture on this particular farm.

## MEETING WITH DOUG FREELANCER

Doug Freelancer's meeting with Captain Upright was scheduled for 9:00 a.m., but was purposefully delayed until 9:16 a.m. This is a tactic in which Captain Upright learned from his days in the Corp. This tactic was used to see if individuals could keep their composure in the anticipation of battle. Mr. Freelancer has been with this particular Farm for three years, has a total of five years of experience in Farming and is a recent college graduate with no prior experience dealing with change in the workplace.

The meeting location is a rustic looking ranch house that embodies the smell of sweat from the profuse labor combined with the soggy heat. In walks Captain Upright, although aged, he has the youth of a thoroughbred and the sharpness of a stallion. His shoes are spit shined and his coat is flawless. Just before entering the ranch house, Captain Upright gives a cigar that he's been smoking and his hat to his trusted assistant, Nathan, a mule that has worked with Captain Upright for twenty-five years in the Farming Industry and is with him to assist with taking notes from the interviews with staff members.

Captain Upright introduced himself to Doug Freelancer and attempted to explain the details of the interview and that the session would last approximately one hour. Doug interrupted and introduced himself and informed Captain Upright, "I will give you anything you need Sir, just let me know, I am very familiar and have the pulse of everything that goes on at this Farm."

Captain Upright thanked Doug and at a second attempt began to explain the details of the interview. This time, with a stern voice, Captain Upright said, "Think of this interview as an assessment of the Farm, we are all aware of the budget cuts and what that means for the employees on this Farm."

After more small talk, the time now is approximately 9:21 a.m. and Captain Upright began to ask questions about the culture on the Farm, "So tell me Doug, what are the employees like on the Farm."

With a smile on his face, Doug stated, "I'm going to change the question Captain, rather than talk about the employees, I prefer to start by detailing some of the changes that I've made on the Farm during my tenure." With a military style stare, Captain Upright interrupted Doug and said, "That's fine Doug, but I'm curious about the employees as a whole."

With a curious look on his face, "What do you mean Captain?" Captain Upright repeated, "I'm here because I'm curious about the employees working together as a whole unit." Doug then started by saying, "That's what I've been trying to tell you, we don't have much of a team chemistry at this Farm, the years that I've been here, I've had to make many changes to the Corporate Farm and most of which was done by researching how things were accomplished on your Farm, Sir." Doug continued to explain, "Also, most of the employees here cannot be trusted and are always requesting time off to deal with personal matters; and there are talks of them even forming a Union with the International Brotherhood of Farmers."

Captain Upright believed in unions since his father was a Chief Steward and had been very successful negotiating matters with management. "There's absolutely nothing wrong with the formation of a union" replied Captain Upright, "Our biggest concern as an International Farming operation is to ensure that the organization is profitable."

Captain Upright turned to Nathan and said, "Take a note of this; we need to take a closer look at what's happening on the Farm, that means better engagement." Growing even more concerned, Captain Upright asked Doug, "Tell me Mr. Freelancer; how did you come across this information." Doug replied, "A little bird told me, Sir". "Seriously, Mr. Freelancer", replied Captain Upright. Doug continued to explain that he was informed by the Farm's Payroll Director, Ms. A. Covert, a bird that doubles as a spy for management, often reporting the habits, gossip and interactions of the employees.

Captain Upright thought that this behavior was quite strange and mentioned, "I know that I am a seasoned employee and perhaps I'm somewhat out of touch with employee engagement; however, I must admit that I too many years ago, when I was a junior manager, spied on employees for upper management, but do you think that it is a good practice to spy on employees?" With a smirk on his face, Doug replied "Absolutely, Sir. In fact, that is one of the things that I've incorporated on this Farm, I encourage spying, I brought this techniques here when I transferred to this Farm from up state because it was very helpful on the other Farms that I've worked on. You see, it gives me an edge up on others."

The time now is 9:43 a.m. and nearing the close of the interview and Captain Upright pulls out Doug's employee evaluation report. "Mr. Freelancer, I've noticed that you've had quite a few stellar years on this Farm with very good ratings. There is one thing that I'd like to know, I noticed that your former supervisor is no longer with the Farm Corp., by chance do you know what happened to him?" Doug replied, "Sure, he wasn't cutting it and let's just say that I had a few meetings with management and he was no longer here after the fact. I really think that we should cut some of the dead weight around here. I'll be honest Sir, these employees are lazy and I always have to take on most of their work."

The time now is 9:51 a.m. and with only a few minutes left in the interview; Captain Upright looks out on the prairie at the animals that are working even more tirelessly than ever and tries to compose his own body language due to the horrendous information that he has been listening to for the past hour. "Doug, one last question, how often do you interact with your colleagues and how often do you interact with management, what's that like?"

Doug explained, "I don't have much in common with my colleagues because they do not have the same educational background that I do. I should be working at one of the exclusive Farms instead of with all of these incompetents. Also, management is not that different from the employees in that they do not understand the business of farming the way that I do, I'm a natural born leader, Sir".

Captain Upright thanked Doug for coming in and explained that he would have a report at the end of his meetings and observations of the Farm. The time now is approximately 10:07 a.m. and as Doug left the office, Captain Upright began profusely documenting information in the report and prepared for his next interview.

Craig Watcher's meeting with Captain Upright was scheduled for 10:30; however, it started later, just as the meeting before with Doug Freelancer. Craig Watcher's meeting started at 10:38 a.m. Mr. Watcher has been with this Farm for twelve years, before transferring in from another Farm. Mr. Watcher also suffers from a medical condition which requires him to be off from work a lot.

The meeting location is the same ranch house; this location will serve as the meeting location for all of the individuals meeting with Captain Upright. It is very hot outside, and the July sun is now beaming down on the ranch house. In walks Craig Watcher, drenched with sweat considering that he's been working all morning conducting his routine duties on the Farm. "Morning Captain, I apologize for my appearance, but it's a rather hot morning and we've got a deadline to reach." The Captain starred at Mr. Watcher for a minute and said, "Not to worry Mr. Watcher, I appreciate a hard worker."

The Captain went on to explain the reasons that he was meeting with the employees on the Farm and explained, "Mr. Watcher, I want to cut to the chase and explain why I am here. As you know, all Corporate Farms have experienced a grave amount of budget cuts and I've been sent here to assess and observe certain practices on this Farm." Captain Upright paused momentarily and began to jot down some questions on his notepad and then turned to Craig, "So, Mr. Watcher, what are the employees like on the Farm?" Looking towards the ground as usual, Craig in a very monotone voice simply said, "Mr. Upright, I'm just a cow on the farm, and my job is to eat the grass."

Captain Upright seemed puzzled and shook his head, thoughtfully, then said, "Mr. Watcher, I appreciate your sincerity, but I really would like to get your opinion as to how you think the employees are on this Farm." Again, Craig stated, "I'm just a cow on the farm, and my job is to eat the grass." Captain Upright said, "Okay, fair enough, so tell me Mr. Watcher how is the management team on this farm?" Craig paused for a second and replied, "I like the management team just fine."

Noticing that the conversation wasn't going anywhere, Captain Upright tried a different approach, " Okay Mr. Watcher, I can tell that you are a bit reserved, I want to assure you that this conversation that we are having is safe and confidential." At this point, Craig could see that Captain Upright was becoming annoyed by his small talk and decided to open up to the interview. "I apologize for my rather to the point comments Captain, but you must understand that it is not easy for employees to communicate with management on this Farm."

Captain Upright appeared quite disturbed at Craig's comments and asked, "What do you mean it is not easy to communicate with management Mr. Watcher?" Craig began to divulge some previous concerns that he had encountered with management on the Farm. "If I may speak freely, I do not wish to get anyone in trouble, but wanted you to know that there's been numerous concerns on this Farm that I've personally brought to the attention of management regarding working conditions and other concerns in which employees are scared to bring to management's attention because they fear that they might lose their jobs."

Again, Captain Upright felt that these comments were quite disturbing and asked Craig to expound on his comments. "Mr. Watcher, in order for me to get a better understanding of the concerns that you've shared with management, please be more specific in telling me about the concerns." Craig paused again momentarily and said, "Captain, I hope that by sharing this information with you that my job isn't in jeopardy." Again Captain Upright assured Craig that the meeting was a safe place.

"I've been on this Farm for twelve years, and during that time, I've witnessed employees come and go and I've seen employees complain to management about numerous things only to see those employees terminated. Now, I cannot prove that they were terminated because they complained to management; however, let's just say that the complainers are no longer employed by this Farm. And this is the reason I decided to sit back and watch things happen rather than to complain about such things. I've even met with and obtained advice from Jerry Wise from the Employee Assistance Program."

Jerry Wise is an owl who works as a Licensed Professional Counselor in the Farm's Employee Assistance Program (EAP) to assist employees who are experiencing stress and ironically, is often stressed himself by all of the overwhelming problems reported by employees; but feels that he cannot help most of the employees because their problems usually falls on deaf ears. Typically when Jerry reports concerns to management, they usually frown upon the information. Also, another source of Jerry's frustration comes from being the only one in the EAP department due to previous budget constraints.

Captain Upright now seemed more puzzled by all of the information that he has learned from some of the employees that he met with in such a short time and replied, "Mr. Watcher, I'm no therapist, but with all of this happening on the Farm, where do you see yourself in the next year?" With hesitation, Craig simply replied, "As I've stated before, "I'm just a cow on the farm, and my job is to eat the grass."

The time now is 11:17 a.m. and it is nearing the end of the interview, "Mr. Watcher, I appreciate the information that you've provided and it is duly noted; however, is there anything else that you would like to add before we adjourn?" Craig looked at Captain Upright for a few seconds with a curious smile and simply said, "I believe that's all that I have to add other than, "I'm just a cow on the farm, and my job is to eat the grass." "Okay Mr. Watcher" replied Captain Upright, "We get the picture." Of note, Craig Watcher is awaiting a hefty settlement from a claim that he filed against the Farm for which he has won. It seems that Craig suffers from an injury that he sustained while working on the Farm; also, he's privy to some of the Farm's wrongdoings and joined a class action lawsuit against the Farm for which he and others are awaiting a decision from the Government.

The time now is 11:35 a.m. "Is there anything else that you would like to add Mr. Watcher?" Craig thought about it for a moment, smiled and said, "No, no, no, I think that about sums it up." Captain Upright thanked Craig for the meeting and jotted down some notes in his binder before breaking for lunch.

## Meeting with Dono Oblivion

After returning from lunch, Captain Upright and Nathan met with Dono Oblivion at the ranch house. Mr. Oblivion is a very curious looking gentleman and has worked on this particular Farm for eighteen years. The time now is 1:06 p.m. and most of the employees have returned to work from their daily lunch break.

On the entire Farm, there is no more a clueless and naïve employee than Dono Oblivion. Although a very hard worker, he wouldn't know if he was being robbed or not. One time there was an employee on the Farm trying to sell a concert ticket because he couldn't go to a concert due to an unforeseen emergency. At the end of the shift when it was time for the employees to go home, this particular employee stood outside of the Farm and held up a sign as other employees were walking by, the sign read: **"RARE BARGAIN, (Concert Ticket) Former Price $40.00, REDUCED TO ONLY $39.98."** In a mad dash, Dono Oblivion, rushed up to the employee and said, "I'm glad that I got to you first before anyone else could purchase the ticket from you, what a bargain! I can't believe that no one else is here but me, wow."

"Mr. Oblivion, my name is Captain Upright, and I would like to meet with you for an hour to discuss the climate on the Farm, if that's okay with you." Dono replied, "Sure Captain Upright, but I want to warn you that unlike Southfork, it's really hot on this Farm." With a curious look, Captain Upright said, "I'm sorry, when I said climate, I was referring to the working conditions and communication styles on the Farm." "Oh, right" replied Dono, "I get confused sometimes."

Captain Upright smiled and continued with the conversation, "So Mr. Oblivion, what are the employees like on the Farm?" Dono's eyes immediately flexed momentarily and with a confused look at Captain Upright and Nathan, he replied, "The employees are great and I love working on the Farm." With an equally confused look, Captain Upright said, "That's great to hear Mr. Oblivion; it's rare that employees are eager to share their feelings about the workplace."

After additional small talk, the time now is 1:37 p.m. and the questions and answers are being exchange rather smoothly between Captain Upright and Dono. Captain Upright pulled out Dono's performance evaluations along with his personnel file and noticed that several employees had filed claims against management on Dono's behalf, considering that they knew that Dono would never stand up for himself even if the evidence was overwhelming. "So Mr. Oblivion, give me your impression of the Farm's Management Team, how do you like their management style?" Dono replied, "I'm happy with their style of management it's rather fashionable." With an even more puzzled look, Captain Upright starred at Dono with astonishment and couldn't believe the responses that he was receiving. "Mr. Oblivion, I notice that several of your co-workers filed claims against Management two years ago on your behalf, could you elaborate or tell me what happened and why you didn't file any of the claims yourself."

Dono paused for a moment in typical confusion and replied, "The reason that I didn't file a claim against management is because I didn't want to get anyone in trouble. I know that they were doing bad things but I am strong and I can take it." The time now is 1:49

and is nearing the close of the interview. "One last thing Mr. Oblivion, since the setback with Management, how's everything thus far, I'm referring to working conditions?" Dono took a sigh of relief because the meeting was almost over, he replied simply, "I'm good." Captain Upright informed Dono that if he needed additional information, he would contact him in the coming days.

After Dono exited the building, Captain Upright and Nathan looked at each other in amazement. Nathan stated, "That's the best comic relief that I've heard in a long time." Captain Upright continued to jot down information for his report and decided that he'd had enough comedy for one day and would conclude the interviews the next day with Ms. Believe.

## MEETING WITH IVANNA BELIEVE

The next day, Ms. Believe's meeting was supposed to have started at 9:00 a.m. but Captain Upright was delayed due to traffic. Ironically, the meeting started at 9:23 a.m. which could be a reference to (Mark 9:23 from the bible). Ms. Believe is a very unassuming lady who is very careful with words and has a very positive outlook on life. She's been in the Farming Industry for sixteen years and has been with the Corporate Farm for seven of those years.

Captain Upright looked at Ms. Believe with an irony of disbelief, due to her enormous height, even while sitting down she stood taller than the Captain and Nathan. "I'm going to start this session a little differently, so tell me about you, what makes you happy?"

Ms. Believe smiled with innocence and replied, "Captain, if you don't mind Sir, I would like to shift that question around some." The Captain sighed for a moment and waited for Ms. Believe to finish, simply replying with "Sure." Again smiling, Ms Believe continued, "Well Sir, I just wanted to say that I really enjoy working on this Farm and most of all, I've come to understand the importance of the

Farming Industry for the world as a whole. Also, I've enjoyed working with my colleagues in assuring that the world is supplied with the needed resources that we produce as a team on this Farm."

Captain Upright's eyebrows lifted and he sat straight up in his chair and even began to smile. You have to understand, Captain Upright is one serious individual and it is very difficult for anyone including his wife to get a smile out of him. "I must say Ms. Believe I'm quite impressed with your feedback, it's not often that employees talk positive about the Farm, please go on, but I'd like to hear something about you, how did you get to this Farm?"

Ms. Believe paused and knew exactly what to say and most of all how to say it. It's as though she was auditioning for a movie role, a chance of a lifetime moment. "Sir, several years ago, I experienced a life altering situation. You see, I was working on a small start up Farm and I was terminated by the owner of the Farm because I wouldn't talk negatively about other Farms in the industry during a routine site visit by the Government. When the owner learned that I refused to say negative things about the competition he immediately terminated me. And although I've had countless opportunities to get even with the owner of that particular Farm, I haven't because I've learned through the years that one must love his enemies, oddly enough, in doing so, makes us all better people. Anyway, when I was terminated, I was really devastated because I'd helped to put that Farm on the map and really wanted to see things flourish. However, instead of being upset and feeling like a victim, I decided to have a campaign of positivity."

At this point, Captain Upright interjected and said, "Ms. Believe, it about 10:12 (a.m.) and although we're coming to the end of the session, would you mind staying longer to finish the story?"

Ms. Believe replied, "Not at all Captain, I was discussing, oh yes, positivity. After crying for a few days, I finally got the negative stuff out of my system and started volunteering my services for free on other Farms in the area. I started to read all about positive materials, journals, books and anything positive that I could get my hands on. A friend of mine gave me a book called *"The Secret"* and it was a life changer, I started reading and applying certain principles in my daily life and it really worked. Also, I read a book called *"Who moved My Cheese"* and it really helped as well because it helped me to cope with change. I also started listening to Pastor Joel Osteen of Lakewood Church, and although I didn't attend any church regularly, Pastor Osteen's message of hope was more about change and how to cope with certain things."

The time now is 10:33 a.m. and the meeting is interrupted by a knock at the door, Nathan opens the door and it's an executive from the office, "Just checking on you guys, I know that you wanted this room for an hour this morning..." Captain Upright explained, "We'll probably need it another hour or so." Nathan closed the door and the executive walked off into the morning mist.

"Well Ms. Believe, I apologize for the interruption, please continue." Ms. Believe now feeling more relaxed because she had heard that Captain Upright was a no non-sense to the minute type of person. "As I volunteered at other Farms, I had to make adjustments in my life and put different priorities in place. I started to get up every morning as though I was going to work on an Executive Farm. One day during a routine visit to the Local Farm by one of the Executives from this Farm, I went out of my way to assist the Executive with setting up meeting rooms, getting coffee, you name it and at the end of the day, that same Executive asked if I wanted to work at one of the Corporate Farms and I was surprised but told him that I couldn't because I was just volunteering and not employed by the Local Farm. The rest is history and I've been working on this Corporate Farm since meeting that Executive. One thing that I'd like to add Captain, life is short and that is why I don't complain, I don't engage in gossip and I work to make this world a better place."

The time now is 11:01 a.m., "What is it that keeps you so positive?" asked Captain Upright. Ms. Believe replied, "I want to let you in on a little secret, my last name wasn't always Believe, I changed it from Skepteaux to Believe after I was terminated. Regarding my positive demeanor, I now know the secret and master key to life. Also, my grandmother used to always tell me the following tale about things that are not always what they seem to be, before I went to sleep every night. The story goes that a pig saw a cow hard at work plowing the land and began to torment the cow by laughing at how much work he had to do. Shortly afterwards, the community was getting ready for their harvest festival, the owner of the Farm released the cow from his chores, but bound the pig with cords and led him away to be slain in honor of the festival. The cow saw what was being done, and said with a smile to the pig, for this you were allowed to live in idleness free from labor, because you are presently to be sacrificed."

The time now is 11:37 a.m., over two hours into the meeting and Captain Upright; now gleaming with enthusiasm, laughter, and excitement exclaims, "Ms. Believe I've never quite heard such a profound story in my life, I too have to let you in on a little secret as well. Many years ago I was very tough on my workers; it was the only way that I knew how to be after I retired from the Corp. I became a very bad manager to the point that my employees didn't like me; however, I had a very abrupt attitude because I didn't care and I kept on getting promoted up the ranks. One day, a colleague of mine who was in management like me, and was just as harsh on his employees as well decided to discipline one of his employees with a written warning for much ado about nothing, I mean this employee; if you ask me, didn't really do anything that would warrant discipline. In hindsight, I think that my colleague should have just communicated with his staff better."

The time now is 11:53 a.m. and there's a sudden pause in Captain Upright's speech and in that moment, the entire room becomes very quiet as Captain Upright becomes somewhat choked up in his speech and then regains composure and starts to repeat the same words. "I was saying that communication is the key, because...because... because that same employee that my colleague disciplined came into work one day and pulled out...pulled out... pulled out a Smith and Wesson revolver and shot and killed my colleague. The employee then took the revolver stuck it in his mouth and then...and then....and then...shot...shot... shot and that was it. That same year, I changed my last name from *Stealing* to *Upright* because from that incident, I learned that life was precious and could be taken away from me in an instant and I've dedicated the rest of my life to living upright. My only regret is that I wish that I could have informed my colleague about changing his ways and becoming a better communicator with his employees. Now, that's not to say that we as executives cannot discipline employees, but that should be the last resort after positive feedback. Ms Believe, I apologize for the duration, but it's been a pleasure speaking with you."

As Ms. Believe stood up, she informed Captain Upright that it was a pleasure as well to have met such an honorable person. Captain Upright closed the door after Ms. Believe left and began to compile all of the information from the interviews to put in his final report.

## Captain Upright's Final Report to the Executive Board

The next morning, Captain Upright completed his final report and emailed it to the Executive Farm for final approval. Due to budget constraints, there was a minor reduction in force, which meant that some of the employees on the Corporate Farm were losing their jobs as expected. Doug Freelancer and Dono Oblivion were among the employees that were affected by the reduction in staff members.

Captain Upright cited that the corporation would fare much better without the likes of an employee such as Doug Freelancer. It was also recommended that Mr. Freelancer not be eligible for rehire once the Farm rebounded from its budget constraints. Dono Oblivion was just a casualty of budget constraints and nothing more. Captain Upright hadn't lasted as long as he did in the workplace without learning a thing or two; even he had to navigate through certain political realities and institutional denial. For example, Craig Watcher remained on the Farm due to his litigious connections which meant that some day he would probably bring the Corporate Farm to its knees. As for Ms. Believe, she was the first female to be promoted to an executive position and ultimately became part owner of one of the Local Farms.

It was also recommended and eventually required that all executives and managers take an accelerated course in conflict management and workplace violence prevention. In addition, executives at the Corporate Farm were required to take communication courses to assist them with disseminating crucial information to staff members.

Captain Upright retired after turning in his final report and moved to Los Angeles, California to spend time with his grandchildren, his real passion for life.

**Believe!**

Believe

# Select Sources

The following sources are by no means a complete record of all the works and sources I have consulted in writing this book, these sources indicates the substance and diversity of my readings and suggestions for those who wish to research further the study and opinions of others on certain subject matter as it pertains to this book:

American Psychiatric Association. (2000). *Diagnostic and Statistical Manual of Mental Disorders* (4th ed., text rev.).

"And Jesus said to him, if you can?' All things are possible to him who believes" (Mark 9:23, New American Standard).

Andersen, H. C. (1837). *Story of the Emperor's New Clothes*. Denmark: C.A. Reitzel. Retrieved from the public domain.

Backstab. 2012. Merriam-Webster.com. Retrieved on September 10, 2012, from http://www.merriam-webster.com/dictionary/backstabbing.

Believe. Dictionary.com. retrieved September 23, 2012, from http://dictionary.reference.com/browse/believe.

Brown, James. (1973). *The Payback* [Recorded by James Brown]. The Payback [Album] Augusta Georgia: International Studios.

Brown, L. (2000). Recording Unknown. Speech presented to an organization.

Bureau of Labor Statistics. (August 16, 2012). *Access to and use of Leave* [Press Release]. Author.

Byrne, R. (2006). *The Secret.* New York: Atria Books.

Culture. 2012. Dictionary.com. Retrieved September 10, 2012, from dictionary.reference.com/browse/culture.

D'Alessandro, D. F. (2008). *Career Warfare.* New York: McGraw Hill.

Death. 2012. Merriam-Webster.com. Retrieved August 31, 2012, from http://www.merriam-webster.com/dictionary/death.

Felkins, Leon. (October 9, 2009 rev). *Political Realities* [online]. Available: perspicuity.net/politics/polreal.html.

Forbes/Forbes Woman (August 8, 2012). *5 Quick Ways You Can Bring Positive Psychology to Your Workplace.* Alexa Thompson.

Giraffe silhouette was used in accordance with all terms and agreements in the free public domain of clker.com.

"Give; and it will be given to you..." (Luke 6:38, New International Version).

Hanks, Tom. (2011). *Larry Crowne*. California: Universal Pictures.

Harvard Business Review (May 29, 2012). *How to Be Happier at Work*. Leonard A. Schlesinger, Charles F Kiefer and Paul B. Brown.

Hurricane Katrina: http://enwikipedia.org/wiki/Hurricane_Katrina.

Johnson, S. (1998). *Who Moved My Cheese?* New York: G.P. Putnam's Sons.

"Keep on asking, and you will receive what you ask for." (Matthew 7:7 New Living Translation).

King, Jr. M.L. (1957, November). *Loving Your Enemies*. Speech presented at Dexter Avenue Baptist Church, Montgomery, Alabama.

Lyubomirsky, S. (2010). *The How of Happiness*: A New Approach to Getting the Life You Want. London: Piatkus.

McFerrin, Bobby. (1988). *Don't Worry Be Happy* [Recorded by Bobby McFerrin]. Simple Pleasures [CD] London, England: EMI.

Meditation: http://en.wikipedia.org/wiki/Meditation.

Moral Compass. Dictionary.com. Retrieved September 10, 2012, from http://dictionary.reference.com/browse/moral + compass.

Muccino, Gabriele. (2006). *The Pursuit of Happyness*. Culver City: Columbia Pictures.

Mulford, P. (2008, original 1889). *Thoughts are Things*. Virginia: Wilder Publications.

Murphy, J. (2011). *The Power of Your Subconscious Mind*. Connecticut: Martino Publishing.

Nightingale, E. (2006 original 1956). *The Strangest Secret*. US: BN Publishing.

Nolan, Christopher. (2008). *The Dark Knight*. Burbank: Warner Bros. Pictures.

Parlette, R. (1988). *The University of Hard Knocks*. Texas: Brownlow.

Plato's Apology: http://en.wikipedia.org/wiki/Apology_Plato.

Reality: http://en.wikipedia.org/wiki/Reality.

Relax. Dictionary.com. retrieved September 18, 2012, from http://dictionary.reference.com/browse/relax.

Rogers, Kenny. (1978). *The Gambler* [Recorded by Kenny Rogers]. The Gambler [Album] Los Angeles, CA: United Artists Records.

Science Daily (April 1, 2010). *Psychologists Search for Secret of Happiness at Work*. Nathan Bowling, Kevin Eschleman and Qiang Wang.

Shaw, Irwin. *Bury the Dead*. New York: Dramatists, 1936. Print.

Sleep. 2012. Merriam-Webster.com. Retrieved August 31, 2012, from http://www.merriam-webster.com/dictionary/sleep.

Substance Abuse: http://en.wikipedia.org/wiki/Substance_abuse.

Tzu, S. (2009). *The Art of War*. London: Arcturus.

Voltaire. (1759). *Candide*. France: Cramer and others.

Wachowski, A., & Lana. (1999). *The Matrix*. Burbank: Warner Bros. Pictures.

Web MD. Better Information Better Health. *Stroke*. 27 July 2012. http://www.webmd.com.

# Notes and Ideas

# Notes and Ideas

# NOTES AND IDEAS

# NOTES AND IDEAS

# NOTES AND IDEAS

# Notes and Ideas

# About the Author

## Shawn P. McCann

Shawn McCann is owner of McCann Consulting and also works as an Employee Relations Professional in the Texas Medical Center in Houston, TX. In addition, he works as a regular Adjunct Professor of Sociology at the University of Houston Clear Lake and is a Professional Mediator. Shawn is a frequent lecturer and holds a Masters Degree in Behavioral Science from the University of Houston Clear Lake. He enjoys traveling, volunteering at non-profit organizations, writing and spending time with his family. He lives with his wife Sara and their children in Houston.